Caretaker Defiance Guide

for Thoughtful Kids

Peter Keuler

Copyright © 2019 Peter Keuler

All rights reserved.

Warning: Although this book appears written logically, many aspects are currently un-scientific. Use at your own risk.

ISBN: 978-1-7331405-0-8 (paperback)
ISBN: 978-1-7331405-1-5 (hardbound)
ISBN: 978-1-7331405-2-2 (larger print paperback)

Contents

Key Word Quick Reference 1
Introduction 7
Different People You Might Meet 9

    The Everything Knower 9
    The Self Guider 12
    The Wise Leader 14
    The Learner 16
    The Worker 17
    The Pretend Everything Knower, Pretend Self Guider,
    or Pretend Wise Leader 19
    The Misguided Person 21
    The Bad Guy 22

Playing With You 24
Helping You 26
Checkboxing Ways 28
How Many to Bother With Your Problems? 33
How Different People Handle
Advantages and Disadvantages 39

    Way 1: Use Their Advantage to Help the Group 40
    Way 2: View People Who Do Not Have That Advantage
    as Less Than the People in Your Group 41
    Way 3: See Your Advantage as Not a Real Advantage 43
    Way 4: All at Once 43

Testing to See What Kind of Person They Are 44

    Testing to See If Someone Is an Everything Knower 44

    Testing to See If Someone Is a Self Guider 45

    Testing to See If Someone Is a Wise Leader 48

    Testing to See If Someone Is a Worker 51

    Testing to See If Someone Is a Pretending Person 53

    Testing to See If Someone Is a Misguided Person 53

    Testing to See If Someone Is a Bad Guy 57

Getting Along With People 59

Reasons to Do or Not Do Something. 59

    Being Naturally Impelled 59

    Being Impelled by Others 61

    Being Limited 66

    For-the-best Limits 69

    Care Control Reasons 72

**How a Learner Could Get Along
With an Everything Knower** 76

How a Learner Could Get Along With a Self Guider 77

How a Learner Could Get Along With a Wise Leader ... 78

How a Learner Could Get Along With Another Learner . 80

    Teasing 80

    Ways of Deciding Who Gets What 84

    Bothering 87

    Threats and Conflict 88

How a Learner Could Get Along With a Worker 92

    A Worker Who Cares for You 94

    Workers Who Don't Care for You 96

    Trying Things Your Way 96

    Trying to Make Workers Happy 99

How a Learner Can Get Along With a Pretending Person . . 100

    Pretending People and Rules 103

    How Often to Give Pretending People Another Chance . 104

    Communicating With Pretending People
    Based on the Damage They Cause You 105

    Can a Pretending Person Be Convinced to Try Other Ways? . . 107

    When Caretakers Take Away Things You Really Need 109

    Getting Along With Someone Who Is Nogentive 114

    Pretending People's Thoughts About You 118

    Talking to Friends About Pretending People 119

How a Learner Could Get Along With a Misguided Person . . 120

How a Learner Could Get Along With a Bad Guy 123

**How Other Types of People Get Along With and
Communicate With Each Other** 124

    How to Get Along With a Worker If You Are a Worker . . . 124

    Pretending Person Getting Along With a Wise Leader . . 124

    Pretending Person Getting Along With
    Another Pretending Person 125

    To be a Wise Leader Who Gets Along With a Learner . . . 125

    How to Get Along With a Wise Leader If You
    Are a Wise Leader 128

Key Word Quick Reference

Advantage	Being in a position that helps you more than other people in a different position. See: Disadvantage, Control over what other people do with their time.
Bad	Something that doesn't help a group of people get along together as well.
Bad Guy	Someone who is happy and thinks it's good when they hurt other people.
Boundary	An imaginary line where people would be sad or upset if you cross it.
Burden Way	Promising to yourself and others that you will help the world a great deal in the future, if you take something that others may need right now. See: Inside Way, Urgency Way, Equal Way, Fair Way.
Care Control Reason	When someone who knows you are a good person says that they will take away things you need to help others, if you don't do what they want.
Caretaker	Someone who closely takes care of one or more other people, usually young Learners. They are so close to those they care for, that they have to find ways to get along with each other.
Control over what other people do with their time	Power. Power over other people. Able to force people to do what you want or having things or experiences other people want. See: Advantage, Impelled by Another.
Defiance	This could mean two things: 1. Doing the opposite of what someone says or causing a ruckus when they try to get you to do what they want. 2. Treating someone as if they are too limited and have too many negative qualities to realize their way or ways aren't good.
Deviant Approach	Continuously breaking a rule someone made for you in order to communicate something to that person. See: Enforce Approach, Mourning Approach, Sneaky Approach, Defiance.
Disadvantage	Being in a position that hinders you more than other people in a different position. See: Advantage, Negative Quality.

Enforce Approach	Trying to keep people following a rule in order to communicate something to whoever made the rule. See: Deviant Approach, Mourning Approach, Sneaky Approach, Impelled by Another.
Enoutable	A quality a person can have. They do everything for a reason that is good, and they can tell you why. The reason they tell you would never be because someone else made them or wanted them to do it. Universally accountable. See: **Self Guider**, Right Setting.
Environment Spaces	A space others take care of for a reason they don't know. The time they spend working on it doesn't make the world a better place.
Equal Way	Splitting up something that people need into equal parts for each person. See: Inside Way, Urgency Way, Fair Way, Burden Way.
Everything Knower	Someone who only does good and knows the past, the future, what everybody thinks, and what's best for everybody.
Fair Way	Splitting up something that people need so that the neediest person gets the most, and the least needy person gets the least. See: Inside Way, Urgency Way, Equal Way, Burden Way.
For-the-best Limit	A reason someone cannot do something for you. It's because they are a good person and know it will not benefit a greater good. They are meant for better things. See: Limit, Impelled by Nature, Impelled by Another.
Freedom	A person's ability to choose how they want to live.
Good	Something that helps a group of people get along better together.
Impelled by Another	Doing what someone else wants you to do because you don't want to get punished. When someone makes you do something. See: Rule, Punishment, Unconventional way to communicate, Impelled by Nature, Limit, For-the-best Limit.
Impelled by Nature	When you do something because your instincts, nature, or your brain really want you to. See: Impelled by Another, Limit, and For-the-best Limit.

Innatured	The quality of a person who is beginning to understand how their actions affect people around them. A person with this quality often changes to fit in with the wishes or needs of others. Formed from the root words *im*mature and **natur**al. See: **Learner**.
Innocent till proven guilty	If someone is accused of a crime, they aren't seen as a criminal until it's proven they did the crime.
Inside Way	Splitting up something that people need, based on what they know about themselves. See: Urgency Way, Equal Way, Fair Way, Burden Way.
Intent	What someone plans to do after they get something. It could be bad or good. See: Burden Way.
Learner	A person who has the potential to help out and do either a bit of good in the future, or even become someone truly great.
Limit	Something someone cannot do even if they wanted to. See: For-the-best Limit, Impelled by Nature, and Impelled by Another.
Misguided Person	A person who harms people around them, and through that harm, they change people to be like them.
Mourning Approach	Accepting a rule and also accepting its bad outcomes, for the sake of communicating something to whoever made the rule. See: Deviant Approach, Enforce Approach, Sneaky Approach.
Negative Label	Remembering and naming someone as a person who did something bad or embarrassing when they were reaching their limits, or had to make a hard decision.
Negative Quality	Something about that person makes them do things that aren't as good for the environment, either because they aren't able to, or they aren't as good a person as they could be. See: Limit, Disadvantage.
Nogentive	A quality of a leader who has trouble working out how a way they support (that isn't their job), which, if everyone supported it, would make the world a worse place to live. See: **Pretending Person**.

Origin Idea	The first idea that guides how someone acts. It could be secret, selfish, hard to communicate, or even forgotten.
Peace	Large groups of people getting along without fighting.
Pocobian	A quality of someone who asks themselves, "If I were being taken care of, could I think of any messages so important, that it would be worthwhile to upset the person I am now, for even a chance to communicate it?" and tends to come up with good answers. Formed from the first letters of the words **P**erson **O**ne **CO**uld **B**e. See: Wise Leader.
Punishment	The bad thing that someone does to you after you break a rule. See: Rule, Impelled by Another, Unconventional way to communicate.
Pretending Person	Someone who acts like they are a great leader who's in control of what they do with their time and tries to hide anything that proves they are not.
Reason	Have a way for someone to convince you that you are wrong.
Reserve Judgment	Not deciding if you like someone or not knowing if something is true until you know more. See: Wise Leader.
Right to Life	The belief that it's good when people are alive.
Rubene	A quality of a leader who asks themselves questions like, "What's wrong with my leadership skills?" more than they ask themselves, "What's wrong with the people I lead?". See: Wise Leader.
Rule	Advice that you have to follow or else someone will punish you. See: Punishment, Impelled by Another.
Self Guider	A legendary person who has done many things in their life and has seen what happens. What they know, they've learned only from first-hand experiences. They do good and don't let anyone stand in their way.
Sneaky Approach	Trying not to get caught when breaking a rule. See: Deviant Approach, Enforce Approach, Mourning Approach.

Specialized	Stop learning about everything and focusing on learning one or two skills to help the world be better. See: **Worker**.
Right Setting	All the things that you have to pay attention to before doing an action is considered good. The specific conditions that makes something OK. Example: You should only put your friend on the moon under the right setting: 1. They are in a spacesuit. 2. It has oxygen. 3. They are not sick. 4. They have a way to get back. 5. They want to go to the moon. (Only a **Self Guider** can tell you all the right settings for everything they do.) See: Enoutable.
Teasing	An unconventional way to communicate (see below) whose messages could be: 1. I'm better than you, or 2. I think you can improve in a way that I don't know how to say in a nice way.
Testing	On people; to try to find out what kind of person someone is by setting up a situation and seeing how they act when it happens.
Unconventional way to communicate	Trying to say something important to someone else with uncomfortable or unpleasant words or actions. See: Punishment, Impelled by Another, Pocobian.
Urgency Way	Splitting up something that people need, so the person who acts like they need it the most gets the most, and the person who acts like they need it the least gets the least. See: Inside Way, Equal Way, Fair Way, Burden Way.
Verse	A person who knows the basics of almost every way of being and every way people could be together. They are always happy to demonstrate their knowledge. Formed from the first few letters from the word "**vers**atile." See: Way, **Self Guider**.
Viewing someone as less than	Seeing someone as less of a person, and not caring too much if they are sad or happy. Not including them as part of your world.

Way	What actions a person sees as good or bad. How a person chooses to feel when they see another person doing something. How someone could live their life and how people could get along together.
Waylock	When someone is unable to change how they feel about something, even if they have good reasons, and is unable to even just try and see how it goes.
Wise Leader	A person who is happy when the people they lead try to make the world a better place and thinks very hard about how to help them do that.
Worker	Someone who is really good at a few things and wants to live a nice normal life. See: Specialized.

Caretaker Defiance Guide, for Thoughtful Kids

Introduction

When is it OK to go against your caretakers? What does it mean to defy them? Sure, a child not doing something healthy at their parents' request might be defiant, but what about hitting someone who pronounces a word differently from your caretakers? Is that defiance or respect? Is thinking that your caretakers have bad qualities, without them letting you know, defiance or respect? What if a parent asks their child to hurt another child? Is obeying them respectful? Is raising your own kids with less hardship than your parents gave you, defiance or respect? Is admitting someone is right, when your caretakers never admitted you were right, defiance? Is giving up hope that your parents are smart enough to try things a different way, defiance? Perhaps defiance is good sometimes, but when?

This guide is split into different sections to help you decide when you should defy someone:

- **"Different People You Might Meet"** lets you know the qualities of the type of people you should always believe in, qualities of the type of people you should never believe in, and everyone in between! (You don't have to remember the names of the qualities, just what they are.)

- The **"Helping You"** and **"Playing With You"** sections help you figure out what each type of person thinks when it comes to playing with and helping someone like you.
- **"Checkboxing Ways"** is to help you figure out who is responsible when you do something bad that you thought was good, and who is responsible when your caretaker does something bad that they thought was good.
- **"How Many to Bother With Your Problems?"** is to help you figure out when you should interrupt others to ask them for help or just keep your problems to yourself.
- **"How Different People Handle Advantages and Disadvantages"** goes over how some people really like helping others when they can, and also how some people decide not to help others even when they can.
- **"Testing to See What Kind of Person They Are"** is a section to help you figure a person out if they don't tell you what they are like, so you can better know how to treat them.
- **"Reasons to Do and Not to Do Something"** is to help you figure out why people might try to stop you from doing something without telling you why.
- Next, there are several sections about how someone like you and your friends can get along with people who are always good to believe in, people that are never good to believe in, and everyone in between!
- Finally, there are some sections about how those sorts of people get along and talk to each other.

Different People You Might Meet

★ The Everything Knower

It's OK to restrain and use force on those who defy their way.

An Everything Knower can think about everything before they make the best decision.

Defining Quality:

- *Knows everything*: Every **way** they use is to achieve their goal of having a good, thriving environment. They are so smart, that they have figured out what **ways** everyone can follow, where bad things start, and where everything could end. They have chosen the best and most ideal ending. If people started using different, less-clever ways, it's not hard to see how things would get more and more out of control, and everything would get worse and worse.

One child loves to get wet and play in the rain. Another is sad and tries to protect themselves from the rain.

Ways are how someone can live their life and get along with others. Different people in different places use different ways. Here are some examples:

- Sometimes people think, "It's OK to get really sad if you get wet in the rain."
- Other times people think, "It's fun to get wet when it rains on you."
- Sometimes people think, "It's OK to feel mad at someone who drives on the right side of the road."
- Other times people think, "It's OK to feel mad at someone who drives on the left side of the road."
- Sometimes people think, "People should say exactly what they mean, and it's their fault if they are not understood. It's OK to be mad at them."
- Other times people think, "What people say is close to what they mean. It's OK to be a little mad at yourself for not double-checking if they are misunderstood."
- Some people think, "If you have a machine that works, it should be shiny."
- Other people think, "It doesn't matter if a machine is shiny, as long as it works."
- Some people think, "It's good to correct someone if they don't spell exactly right."
- Other people think, "It's good to not mind if someone doesn't spell right, as long as you understand."
- Some people think, "It's good to only use someone's invention for what it's made for."
- Other people think, "It's good to use inventions in interesting, and perhaps useful, new ways outside of what they are made for."

Someone yells at a child for not using chairs and blankets for what they are made for. Another person is quite proud of them.

Sometimes it is very difficult to find out when ways are good and when ways are bad. One way that seems bad might be good when combined with another way. Even a way that seems good for one person may end up being very bad if a large group of people use it. An **Everything Knower** knows the result of every combination of ways, and since they're nice, they will already have chosen the best ones.

A very hard one would be figuring out which side of the road is best for everyone to drive on. An **Everything Knower** would consider: How many people are right handed or left handed? Does it even matter? Which side is safer? Which side do people new to driving think is best? Which side will be faster? And there are many, many other things to think about.

Dealing with an **Everything Knower** is pretty simple. Do whatever they tell you because it's for the best, since they already know exactly what effect their words and actions have on you. If you see someone going against their way, it's OK to try to stop them sometimes, by pushing, pulling, or even hitting them to make them stop.

If they didn't know everything, they would surely tell you, but since they do, there is nothing to tell. If they didn't know the best ways to do things, they would try other ways, but since they don't try other ways, they must have already found the best way.

Unfortunately, no such person exists now or has ever existed on record. It might take hundreds of years to find out if it's even possible for such a person to exist. It would be highly recommended to prepare for other types of people.

While there may be no individual person whose ways are worth fighting and hurting others for, lots of people think, "If I was as smart as an **Everything Knower**, then I would know some ways are worth fighting for." Ways like, "It's good to keep people free" (**Freedom**) and "It's good when people are alive" (**Right to Life**).

★ The Self Guider

It's OK to only think in ways they provide for you and try to get others to use their way.

Someone tries to stop a Self Guider from doing what they want (which is always the right thing), but it is no use. Other people cannot stop Self Guiders from doing what's right.

Defining Qualities:

- *Enoutable*: *Every way they choose is their own decision and for the good of all.* If they do something, they have a very good reason for it that they can tell you. They may not know if it's for the best, but completely intend to find out. They would never do things a certain way for unknown reasons. They would never do things a certain way because they are afraid of what someone else would do to them. They would never do things a certain way just because everyone else does it that way. They would never do something to look better for someone else whom they depend on or need something from.

- *Verse*: *They are good at anything they try.* They know the basics of almost every way of being and almost every way people could be together. Not *Verse*: "I don't like that." *Verse*: "I tried that and found out I didn't like it, but in trying it, I got a little good at it. Here, let me show you." A person who is very *Verse* can surely get along in a city where stealing and tricking is OK, and surely get along in a city where everyone is honest and shares everything, or even a city where people say hi by dancing like a chicken.

A Self Guider is very good at just about anything, even embarrassing things like chicken dancing to say hi.

Dealing with a **Self Guider** is pretty nice too. All you have to do is think in the ways they provide you, and if there's a problem, they will take responsibility for it. They will change their ways to account for it. If they feel a certain way about something, you know that there is a good reason and that it's OK to feel the same about it. You can always ask them why they do the things they do and can expect to get a good answer.

Everything they say is very well considered. You can spend a lot of time thinking about the meaning of their words. Everything that they have to say is steeped in their great wisdom and wealth of experience. Their simplest phrases have been considered and constructed most carefully.

You can push their ways further and also extend their ways into other areas of life. You can imagine how well a group of people would get along if everyone did things their way. Everything they like is something that could likely make for a better world. Everything they do and everything they show you is something they like!

Their ways are worth spreading to other people who don't know about them yet. Having more people follow their way helps a **Self Guider** more quickly figure out if it's best. It helps them get closer to becoming an **Everything Knower**. If they are doing something that is bad and harms you, it's OK because they will realize it and then do something else (maybe even try one of your ideas!). Even if they continue to use a way that keeps you from being your best, it's still OK. They will realize it has hindered you then try something else with the next person or group they care for.

It's never a waste of time to try convincing a **Self Guider** that a way they support isn't good for the world. They will be happy to know. And if you convince them, they will then defy this way right alongside you!

Unfortunately, like an **Everything Knower**, no one has known a **Self Guider** to exist. No one knows for sure if it's even possible for such a person to exist. It is recommended that you prepare yourself for other types of people.

There may be no individual whose ways are worth replacing over other people's ways. However, lots of people think that if they or someone else was as smart as a **Self Guider**, they would know some ways are worth spreading. Ways like, "It's good for families or groups to work out problems without hurting each other" (**Peace**), "It's good to have a way anyone could convince you to change" (**Reason**), and "It's good to not blame someone for a bad thing that happened unless you have proof" (**Innocent Until Proven Guilty**).

★ The Wise Leader

It's OK to do things that they think are good (do things that would impress them).

Defining Qualities:

As destruction unfolds in front of the *Wise Leader*, they wonder what they have or have not done that may have caused all this to happen.

- *Rubene*: A leader who is so smart, they recognize and understand that the end behavior of their subjects is mostly a result of the actions, policies, and example they provide. They don't think it's because something might be wrong with their subjects. They are so wise, they can even understand which of their past actions resulted in the actions of their subjects months, years, and possibly decades later. They keep these results in mind when they change how they act for the next group of subjects.

- *Pocobian:* A person who asks themselves, "What kind of messages would be so important that it would be worth upsetting myself or someone else for even a chance to communicate it?" and tends to come up with good answers. They use these answers to further guide their actions. They assume the messages are about topics related to all aspects of self-improvement – principles like: doing your best, what's best for making a thriving environment, justice, fairness, freedom, self-protection, a desire to communicate better, valid needs, valid frustrations, best use of time/resources, peace, war, and more.

A child is frustrated at a Wise Leader and kicks them. The Wise Leader just stands there and thinks about what important messages the child might want to tell them.

Dealing with a Wise Leader is also nice. You can do things independently. They may not understand what you do, but they know that it could prove to be good or useful someday. Even if you make a mistake or it doesn't turn out great right away, it's still OK!

They wonder what sort of guidance you need and how to give it to you. If you try things their way and you have a frown on your face because you are sad, they take note of it, and then accept that you are sad. They wouldn't want you to pretend that you aren't sad. They like to talk about whether something is working for you or not.

They have almost everything planned out and if one of their plans goes wrong in the future, they usually have a plan on how to handle that.

They may not do everything for a reason like a Self Guider, but if they do something that affects others, then they probably do have a reason for that.

There are very few Wise Leaders in the world. Many people go through life never even meeting one! If you prepare yourself to meet one and you never do, it would be a waste of time and energy. If you don't prepare yourself to meet one, it will make it harder for them to help you if you get lucky and meet one (if you have a friend, just one of you could prepare to meet one, so you can both be ready for whatever happens).

★ The Learner

It's OK to do things that would impress the person they want to be and it's also OK not to trust them to respond well to your actions.

A Learner realizes they are unable to color inside the lines now, but somehow knows for sure they will be able to with enough practice.

Defining Qualities:

- *Discovering Limits: They are trying to improve themselves. They are honest with themselves when they discover limits and think about how to overcome them.*

- *Innatured: Beginning to understand how their actions could affect people around them. They often wonder what they have done to cause someone to feel a particular way.*

Dealing with a **Learner** can be lots of fun because you can both share the progress you make, be confused together, and see each other grow. Since they don't know much yet, they are open to trying new ideas and seeing how they work.

Sometimes it isn't fun. If you get tired of trying to think about what to do and ask them what to do next, they might not know either. Showing them how committed you are to their way is no good because they try switching ways a lot. They may not know how to treat you after you impress them.

Some **Learners** are very selfless. If they find the right cause, they will give all they have for it and are very happy to help.

If you tell a **Learner** that you believe something that doesn't quite sound right (like something is impossible or can't be done) they are happy to spend a lot of time proving you wrong to help you.

They might often say or act like someone different from how they used to be. If you treat them as if they are that new sort of person, it helps them figure out if it's good or not. They often feel the need to try their absolute best at doing things a particular way, just to make extra sure it does or it doesn't work. If it doesn't, they'll usually switch.

There are lots of **Learners** in the world!

Exercise: On another piece of paper, write down the letters of the actions that you think are **innatured**.

A. A kid accidentally bumps into some people when he goes to the store. The next time, he watches where he is going more carefully.

B. A **Learner's** parent accidentally keeps leaving the stove on and burning the food. The next time, the **Learner** reminds the parent that there is food on the stove so it won't burn.

C. A person pronounces french fries, "frank forts" when he orders food, and the restaurant messes up the order. This keeps on happening at every restaurant they go to.

D. A boy and a girl are on an airplane chatting. The boy asks the girl, "Where do you live?" The girl says, "In my house." The next time the boy chats with someone, he says, "What country do you live in?"

E. A lady is driving on the opposite side of the road to everyone else and keeps on honking at people who are coming at her. The next day, she does the same thing again.

F. A little girl wants her father to just look at a toy, so she hands it to him. He says, "Thanks," and puts it on his shelf (he thought she was giving it to him). The next time she wants him to look at a toy, she holds it up and points to it.

Answers: these ones are innatured: A, B, D, F

*A **Learner** holds up an interesting toy and points to it, as if she's saying that she wants her dad to just look.*

★ The Worker

It's OK to do things that would impress someone else, and it's OK not to trust them to respond well to your actions.

Defining Quality:

- *Specialized:* They have stopped trying to develop into leaders because they aren't smart enough to grow further, or they have decided to leave it to someone else. They now focus on a particular job or jobs to benefit the world. They use the ways that others use without understanding why or what effect it has on them and the world, but they assume it's good. Whether it is good or not is something they don't like to talk or think about.

Dealing with a **Worker** can be fun. They might be very good at what they do, and it's fun to watch them.

Workers have come a long way. They each learn one or two jobs to make the world a nicer place to live, if they work together.

It can sometimes be frustrating. If you try to show them that you believe in them a lot, they may not realize it or know how to handle it. If you wish to be the kind of person others can believe in, looking at their example won't help. If you try to show them how much their ways are hurting you, they may also fail to recognize it. It has never been their way to spend a lot of time thinking deeply and considering carefully the reasons behind different actions or outcomes in life. Their views on the world can be very simple and half finished.

Sometimes they do things they don't like because someone has forced them to. They may much prefer to do something else. Some examples of things they don't like, but do anyway: paying taxes, going to work, picking up after other people, and following the rules.

Also, if they show something to you, they might not actually like it themselves. They may be just showing you to impress someone else. They may not actually care if you like it or not. Some examples of things they show you that they don't actually like: watching shows about sharing and caring, rules about paying attention for a long time, getting every answer right on a test about swamps.

Sometimes they like things that are suitable for a **Worker** to like, but not a **Wise Leader**. They might pretend to dislike these things when you are around so that you have a better chance of being a **Wise Leader**. Things like watching too much TV, eating too much junk food, yelling at people on TV, using bad words, or something else.

In their spare time, they may care for a space like a Leader would take care of a group of people. Since they don't lead an accountable life, they don't know exactly why they do it. Maybe it helps them think more clearly and be at peace. Perhaps they want to know how the people who rule them feel. Doing things like tending to a garden, taking care of pets, caring for objects, maintaining their home, or tending to a virtual environment are examples of what they would do. They know they may be unsuited for larger tasks.

Sometimes they treat their **Environment Spaces** like they are a real, thriving space, just like a Mayor would treat their city. They get very distressed if it breaks – like a Mayor would if part of the city broke and people got hurt. They follow the way of: "If you put a lot of time into something, other people should be careful with it," without thinking about why they do it, or if it could be used for good or not. The world is full of **Workers**!

★ The Pretend Everything Knower, Pretend Self Guider, or Pretend Wise Leader

It's OK to do things that would impress someone else, and it may be a good idea to try a way that is the opposite of theirs, and to keep some secrets from them.

Defining Qualities:

- *Deceptive: They are pretending they Act for the Good of All, Know Everything, Do Everything for a Reason, and/or Keep Track of Their Actions and the Effect of Those Actions.* They may pretend their ways are their own, but they come from lots of places. Their ways could be outdated, bad for the world, or created for selfish reasons. They think about how to hide the secret that they are not whom they pretend to be *more* than they think about how to become a better person.

- *Nogentive: A nogentive person is a leader who has trouble working out how a way they and their followers collectively support would make the world a worse place to live.* Imagine a pond with limited fish; **Nogentive** people would keep on fishing in it until there are none left and wouldn't stop and wait until there were more fish. **Nogentive** teachers would not be willing to admit it would be better if "island" was spelled "iland" to save ink and be easier for beginners to read.

Someone tells their children how much he likes the nice park, while also throwing garbage on the ground. If everyone did that, the park would be filled with garbage and not be nice anymore!

Dealing with a Pretend **Self Guider**, Pretend **Everything Knower**, or Pretend **Wise Leader** can be very complicated and difficult. You will probably have to spend some time away from thinking about how you can do good, and a lot of time trying to figure out:

- If someone is pretending.
- What to do once you discover that they are pretending.
- Figure out the reason for their pretending:
    - because they are bad and make mischief on purpose
    - because they want to play a pretending game with you
    - because it is a joke
    - because that is all they know
    - because their survival or that of their family depends on it
    - because they wanted to keep an even worse **Pretending Person** from becoming a leader

You'll also have to think about:

- If (since you last saw them) they have come to realize the negative effect of their ways and decided to change.

- How often to give them another chance to realize that being a **Pretending Person** isn't good.

- Which of their ways are bad and worth doing the opposite of, and which of their ways might still be good and worth keeping.

- Which ideas and experiences you can share with them and which ones you can hide from them because they will use that information to hinder your ability to do good.

They might be much more suited for tending to a garden, pets, a virtual environment, and other types of environment spaces, instead of leading people. If their ways hinder the people they lead, they have a hard time realizing it and continue to damage them and their ability to do good. Even though they are such a difficulty and hindrance to others, many of them genuinely believe their ways are for the best, and they are just trying to be good.

There are many **Pretending People** in the world. There are currently no rules against pretending (many people follow the way of: "It's good to admire deceptive qualities"). It would be recommended to prepare yourself for them.

★ The Misguided Person

It's OK to resist them if they try to force you to follow their ways.

Defining Quality:

- *Changer*: *They try to forcefully change others from a person who does good.* They won't be able to explain why their way is good, and it most likely isn't anyway. They can do very unexpected things to confuse you and act like they are normal, so you think it's normal. They have the easiest time doing this to young **Learners**, because they don't know much about the world yet.

Dealing with a **Misguided Person** is very unpleasant. They cause good people discomfort until they become like them. Perhaps someone in the past hurt them so much that they forgot who they were, and they now think that hurting people in the same way is OK. Maybe they are worried that other people might grow to have control over what they do with their own time. Perhaps they wish to hurt others so they can stay in control.

Here are some unpleasant things **Misguided People** might think are OK to do to others:

- Hitting people who disobey them.
- Taking away a **Learner's** food if they don't do what they are told.
- Shouting at a **Learner** and asking them why they are playing with something.

- Lying to people about how the world works so they do what the **Misguided Person** wants.

Unfortunately, there are many **Misguided People** in the world. There are some rules against having **Misguided People** spread their ways to others, but not many. Some ways you might think should be well known as bad are *still* considered good! Oh, no! It would be recommended to prepare for them a bit.

★ The Bad Guy

It's OK to hold them back or use force on them when they use their ways.

Defining Quality:

- **Bad**: *They intend to cause harm to good or potentially good people and their environment.* They wish to only take things for themselves and don't care how much harm it causes others. They may even enjoy causing others harm.

Even seeing a **Bad Guy** (or Bad Person) is scary. They like to greedily take things away from people who are very needy, hurt people whom they don't like, and even kill innocent people. Unlike other types of people, they don't think about all the good that children could do one day. It would be a bad idea to go to them for help.

Since their goals are not good, they do not care how much good you might grow up to do. You should fight them if they want you to do something and call the police if you see one being bad.

Unfortunately, there are still several **Bad Guys** in the world, but a lot less than there used to be, and they are still decreasing. Where we live, there are lots of rules against being very bad. You can trust most people to keep you safe from **Bad Guys** – even a **Pretending Person** or a **Misguided Person** could put a lot of effort into helping you.

- Even if a **Self Guider** saves you from a **Bad Guy**, you still should not fight people who use ways that are different from theirs.

- Even if a **Wise Leader** saves you from a **Bad Guy**, it's still a good idea not to think in only the ways they give you.

- Even if a **Learner** saves you from a **Bad Guy**, it's still OK to do things that would impress the person they want to be (not the person they are now) and not trust them to always respond well to your actions.

- Even if a **Worker** saves you from a **Bad Guy**, it's still OK to do things that would impress someone else, and to not trust them to respond well to your actions.

- Even if a **Pretending Person** saves you from a **Bad Guy**, it's still OK to try some ways that are opposite to theirs, do things that would impress someone else, and keep some information from them (even if they say that you owe them for saving you).

- Even if a **Misguided Person** saves you from a **Bad Guy**, it's still OK to resist them if they try to force you to have bad ways (even if they say you owe them for saving you).

- Even if a **Bad Guy** saves you from another **Bad Guy**, it's still OK to use force against them if they are doing something very bad (even if they say that you owe them for saving you).

Playing With You

An **Everything Knower** or a **Self Guider** who cares for you will want to play with you and they will know how.

A **Wise Leader** or a **Learner** who cares for you will want to play with you and try things your way. They will want to play for you both to discover each other's limits and weaknesses. They might not be very good at it, but it doesn't bother them to try. If someone plays with you but isn't very good at it, they might be a **Wise Leader** or a **Learner**.

A **Worker** who cares for you will play with you to understand each other's limits. They might not put much energy into trying things your way. No matter how much effort you put into playing with them the way they like, no matter what you do to try to impress them, they might never play with you the way you want them to. Instead, they might really enjoy teaching you how to do things their way.

A **Pretending Person** will act like they'll be willing to play with you if you impress them enough. They might pretend they know how to play with you your way, but, if they try, they will be very bad at it. They can never do it because they like to think they are good at everything. Also, they may not want you to find out that they aren't actually that great. They may never want to try things your way, no matter what you do!

A **Misguided Person** believes doing things their way is the only correct way. They may never want to play with you either.

A **Bad guy** who cares for you will never genuinely play with you. They might pretend to want to play with you to trick you because they want something from you.

Exercise: Match the response to whom it describes. Write down which letter goes to which number on another piece of paper.

Imagine you are sitting with your caretaker, not really doing anything. You turn to them and say, "You are a sponge monster." How would each person respond to it?

1. **Self Guider**   A. Is happy that you think they're good enough to handle that sort of challenge. They try to act like a "Sponge Monster" but make some mistakes (like getting too wet and being unable to move) – but it's still fun.

2. **Wise Leader**   B. Gets mad at you for calling them a name and takes away something that you like.

3. **Worker**   C. Gets a little confused and says something but you can't really hear them.

4. **Pretending Person**   D. Gets really mad at you and hits you and yells at you for calling them a name.

5. **Misguided Person**   E. Welcomes a new challenge of viewing the world like this "Sponge Monster" creature. They think really hard and start acting like one. It looks like they have such a good handle on the ins and outs of being a sponge monster that they act like they have lived as a sponge monster for years!

Answers: 1 To F; 2 To A; 3 To C; 4 To B; 5 To D

Helping You

Each type of person you might meet has different thoughts before they decide to help you and give you things:

An **Everything Knower** would think, "I know this person deserves to get what they need to be happy."

A **Self Guider** or **Wise Leader** would think, "I don't know if this person will be a very good person in the future. It would be unfortunate if they become a great person and don't get what they need to be happy, so I will give it to them."

A **Worker** would think, "Making this person happy makes me feel happy, so I will make them happy."

A **Pretending Person** might sometimes think like a **Worker** and help others to feel happy, and sometimes they might think, "I know this person deserves it," without knowing everything about you.

A **Misguided Person** might think, "I should help this person because I don't want to go to jail and I don't want people to hate me."

A **Bad Guy** might think, "I will not get this person what makes them happy because I like being bad."

Exercise: Match the response to what kind of person would do it. Write down which letter goes to which number on another piece of paper.

Imagine you are with your caretaker and you want a toy from another child. They take it from the other child and give it to you. Why would each kind of person do that? What life lesson would a young person learn because of it?

1. **Everything Knower**   A. Doesn't want to see you sad, and the other child doesn't mind too much, so they give you the toy.

2. **Wise Leader**   B. Knows it is more good for you to have the toy than the other child because they know the future. You now learn it's OK to take things from others for yourself.

3. **Worker**   C. Thinks you should get all the toys as long as they are taking care of both of you. You learn that you should take things for yourself when you have a chance.

4. **Pretending Person**   D. Thinks that you deserve the toy more because everything that goes wrong in the world is the other child's fault somehow. You learn it's OK to blame the other child for mistakes you make.

5. **Misguided Person**   E. They often take toys from kids just to see them cry. You learn it's OK to like being mean to people.

6. **Bad Guy**   F. Thinks everyone should get equal time to play with a toy, so both of you get a chance to be your best. You know the way of sharing is good this time.

Bonus question: How many **Everything Knowers** are there in the world? How would they let you know?

A. One: my caretaker.

B. Maybe there could be one, but probably not my caretaker. I will treat them like they are one and wait until they tell me themselves.

C. None. My caretaker probably isn't smart enough to tell me they aren't one, unless I'm *very* lucky and have a **Wise Leader** as a caretaker. I should plan on what to do if they never tell me (so it's not good to take things from others for yourself).

Answers:
1 To B; 2 To F; 3 To A; 4 To C; 5 To D; 6 To E
Bonus Question Answer: C

Checkboxing Ways

Sometimes, to make progress, you need to use a bunch of different ways. But, trying to remember why some ways are good in the first place could slow you down. To do the most good, you might have to forget why you do things in a particular way. Sometimes, forgetting can cause difficulties too.

✓	Eating Food	**...status?**	Good
✓	Sharing toys	**...status?**	Good
✗	Eating mud	**...status?**	Bad
✗	Swimming in hot lava	**...status?**	Bad
✓	Swimming in hot lava if you're a lava monster	**...status?**	Good

This lava monster thinks it's good to swim in hot lava and invites a Learner to join him. The Learner knows it's only good if you are a Lava Monster.

Thinking about what's **good** and **bad**, and **right** and **wrong** is really hard for most people. It can be really hard to work out which action is best in the **right setting**. Usually, people let someone else do the thinking for them if they are unable to handle it.

Different kinds of checkboxes:

Type of Checkbox	Who Uses It
• I have tried every different way possible and found this one to have the best outcome.	**Everything Knower**, **Self Guider**, **Wise Leader**, **Learner**
• I have tried every different way I could think of and found this to have the best outcome.	**Self Guider**, **Wise Leader**, **Learner**
• I put a great deal of thought into this and considered lots of options and chose this way.	**Self Guider**, **Wise Leader**, **Learner**, **Worker**
• I put a little thought into this way, and I saw lots of other people doing it, and I'm sure at least one of them figured out if it's good and can explain why.	**Learner**, **Worker**, **Pretending Person**, **Misguided Person**
• After playing around with this, I completely understand how it works, and now I can use it. I can re-explain it instantly if I need to.	**Everything Knower**, **Self Guider**, **Wise Leader**, **Learner**, **Worker**
• After playing around with this, I understand how this works, and now I can use it. I do not need to remember how I came to understand how it works. I'm sure I could figure it out again if I need to.	**Wise Leader**, **Learner**, **Worker**, **Pretending Person**
• Someone whom I trust as an **Everything Knower** chose this way. It must be good.	**Wise Leader**, **Learner**, **Worker**, **Pretending Person**, **Misguided Person**
• Someone whom I trust as a **Self Guider** chose this way. It must be good.	**Wise Leader**, **Learner**, **Worker**, **Pretending Person**, **Misguided Person**
• Someone whom I trust as a **Wise Leader** chose this way, and after trying it myself, I also found it to be good.	**Wise Leader**, **Learner**, **Worker**
• I had a nice moment with a friend doing things this way, so it must be good.	**Learner**, **Worker**, **Pretending Person**, **Misguided Person**

- Doing things this way makes me feel good, and doesn't harm anyone. I usually like things that are good, so this must be good too. **Learner**, **Worker**, **Pretending Person**, **Misguided Person**

- Doing things this way makes me feel good, but it harms others. That's always OK. **Misguided Person**, **Bad Guy**

If you can't remember why you decided to checkbox a certain way, at least try to remember what **type** of checkbox it was. If you want to improve yourself, you can go back and think it through again. If someone you looked up to wasn't who you thought they were, then you know you might want to rethink the ways they have given you.

In this world, our current way is "hold children and people who aren't in charge responsible for what they do." Therefore, if someone leads a child to do something, the leader will usually not be responsible at all.

- If you had a nice moment doing things a certain way with a friend, and then you do it by yourself, and it turns out to be not a good action, then your friend won't be held responsible. Examples: hurting people younger than you, making fun of someone who needs help, petting ferocious alligators.

*The **Learner** remembers last time he and his friend had a nice time petting ferocious alligators together. Doing it now must be good too, right?*

- If you saw lots of other people doing something a certain way, and it turns out to be a bad action, then you will still be held responsible for your actions. Examples: breaking something that someone worked hard on, calling someone a name they don't like.

- If someone you trusted does something in a way that turns out to be bad, they will not be responsible if you do it.

Examples: If you see your parents yell at everyone who tries to help them (like waiters or car mechanics), or you see your boss hitting people who are disobedient, and you repeat any of these actions in situations of your own, then you will be held responsible.

Also, in this world, our current way (and the way of **Workers**, **Pretending People**, **Misguided People**, and some **Learners**) is "it is OK for grownups to *not* hold themselves responsible for some ways that they treat kids."

An older Learner convinces a young Learner to throw rocks at a building. The young Learner realizes we live in a world where it's everyone's fault if something turns out to be bad, even though most young Learners are born wanting to do things with other people.

- If they treat you in a way that is taken from someone they trust as a **Self Guider**, they will not feel responsible for anything bad that happens because of it. Example: if a teacher or principal tells your parent to do something to you that hurts more than it helps, your parent will not feel responsible if it's discovered that the action hurt you.
- If they treat you in a way that they have put little thought into, and have seen lots of other people treating kids like that, they will not feel responsible if it's actually bad. Example: If every parent has their children play at certain times of the day, instead of when the child wants to, your parents will not feel responsible if it causes some harm.

Different people have different ideas about how to get you to rethink your ways:

An **Everything Knower** might not ask you to rethink your way, they might just tell you to do things a different way.

If a **Self Guider** asks you to rethink your way, you know that they certainly thought really hard and have some experience doing things that way, and found it to be bad. They will probably tell you a story of how they discovered this.

Wise Leaders rarely ask you to rethink your way – they do not know enough about you or anything else to be able to do that. They might ask you to rethink your way if yours is dangerous. If you gave their way a try, they would be very interested to know if it worked or not.

If a **Learner** asks you to rethink your way, you can give it a try and let them know. They will hopefully want to take turns rethinking things if you ask them to.

If a **Worker** asks you to rethink your way, it may be because they do not know what to say, and they are uncomfortable with silence, so they just said that. You can give it some thought, but not too much. Definitely don't give it more than twice as much thought as they give your own ways.

A **Pretending Person** would ask you to rethink your way like an **Everything Knower**. Be careful! They probably don't actually know that much. They will not be willing to rethink theirs if you ask them. They think that their checkbox of "It helps me feel good, and doesn't harm anyone, and I usually like things that are good, so it must be good," is better than everyone else's. They think other people should put a lot of time into rethinking their ways, but never do the same themselves. If you try their way and report back that it did not work for the best, they might not believe you. For some **Pretending People**, there is almost nothing you can do to convince them that their way is not the best for making a good thriving environment.

In this age on Earth, if there was a rule that said, "Everyone who decides to be a leader who *isn't* accountable for all their actions (a **Self Guider**) has to go to jail," then *every* parent, boss, teacher, and president would have to go to jail! That rule might be a good idea if there were several **Self Guiders** in the world, but not right now.

Unless someone is pretending to be a **Self Guider**, try not to get too mad at them if they use a way but don't know why. Since there are no known **Self Guiders**, probably everybody does it sometimes – perhaps even including you, and that's OK. They can improve on their own, hopefully.

How Many to Bother With Your Problems?

Most of the time, you should treat everyone the best you can. Imagine you have enough food to share with four people. Three of them are **Learners**, and one is a **Bad Guy** behind bars in jail. You should still let the **Bad Guy** have the food because they can't hurt anyone and there is enough for everyone.

Sometimes there aren't enough resources for everyone. This world isn't currently set up to make everyone comfortable. Now you need to decide: how many **Misguided People** should you upset to make a **Learner** happy? How many **Bad Guys** should you take time to help, over a person who is **Pretending**?

Usually, **Workers**, **Learners**, and **Wise Leaders** follow these guidelines (but there may be lots of other things to consider when making decisions):

The "4s Guideline": How many of a certain type of person is it OK to upset?

You can upset:	To make:	Happy
No one	⟹	1 Bad Guy ☺
4 Bad Guys ☹☹☹☹	⟹	1 Misguided Person ☺
4 Misguided People ☹☹☹☹	⟹	1 Pretending Person ☺
4 Pretending People ☹☹☹☹	⟹	1 Worker ☺
4 Workers ☹☹☹☹	⟹	1 Learner ☺
4 Wise Leaders* ☹☹☹☹	⟹	1 Learner ☺
4 Self Guiders* ☹☹☹☹	⟹	1 Wise Leader ☺
4 Everything Knowers ☹☹☹☹	⟹	1 Self Guider ☺

- If you had to choose between respecting a **Wise Leader** or four **Pretend Wise Leaders**, you would choose the **Wise Leader**.
- If four **Wise Leaders** were playing, it's OK for one or more **Learners'** play to interrupt the play of the **Wise Leaders**.
- If 16 **Pretending People** were playing, it's OK for one or more **Learners'** play to interrupt the play of the **Pretending People**.
- If up to 64 **Everything Knowers** were having a normal meeting, it would be OK for one hungry child to interrupt their meeting to ask for some food.

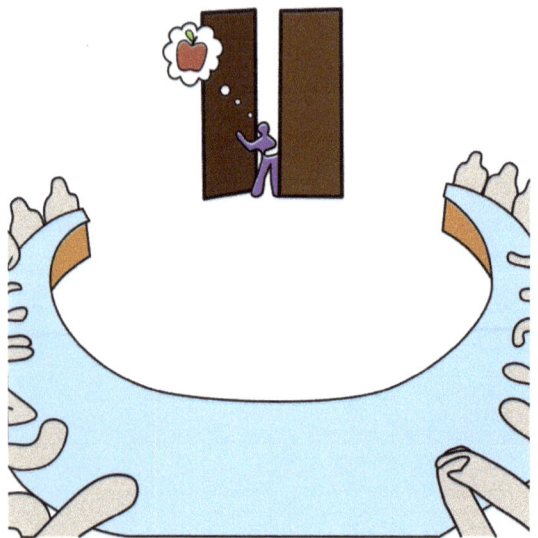

A *Learner* interrupts a meeting of many *Everything Knowers* to ask for some food. The *Everything Knowers* would be sad if she didn't.

These are just guidelines. That means you shouldn't follow them closely all the time. Here are some things that may also be acceptable:

- Keep on doing things that would upset a **Worker**, but would make a **Wise Leader** feel welcome and trusted.
- Frustrate more than 16 **Pretending People** for a **Learner**.
- Four **Learners** switching to a quiet game so a tired **Worker** can rest more peacefully.
- A **Learner** trying hard not to disturb a **Worker** who needs to focus on helping their boss, who is a **Wise Leader**. They are doing something very important that could do a lot of good.
- Not playing near a **Pretending Person** who is known to hurt your ability to do good if you upset them too much with your play.

- Let two **Learners** upset 40 **Pretending People**, if the only way to stop them is to hurt them.

***Self Guiders** and **Wise Leaders'** life mission is to help others, so bad or inconvenient things that happen to them don't bother them too much. Things that truly upset a **Wise Leader** or **Self Guider** are things that affect many others. You should pay attention not to do anything that would upset them in a way that affects others. Upsetting them could mean many innocent people also get upset. But, don't worry too much, they are very good at communicating **boundaries** and when it's OK for you to take up their time.

Workers often get confused about what to put energy into. Sometimes, they would readily upset lots of **Learners** just to make themselves feel a little better. Other times, they would give a great deal of time and energy to help just one **Learner** a little bit. To be nice to them, you should make sure you only ask them for help with things that would really help you become your best. They can't tell what would help you and what wouldn't.

Workers are also very confusing regarding when they think you should ask for help and when not. They might get upset if you don't tell them when something is making you a bit uncomfortable, but when you tell them something is making you *very* uncomfortable, they might get mad or upset at you for complaining about it. Sometimes, their ways can be very unpredictable, and they don't realize it.

A Learner is seen with an injury on her arm. A Worker overly reassures the Learner that she can ask the Worker for help whenever she feels bad. A bit later, the Learner is wearing shoes that are too tight and are hurting her feet. She comes to the Worker for help, but the Worker yells at her instead of helping.

Sometimes, **Pretending People** and **Misguided People** may act very upset if they don't get to have an experience they want. But even if they did get their way, it would not benefit them. Unlike **Learners**, who improve when they have an experience and learn from the result, **Pretending People** and **Misguided People** have a very hard time learning new things. That is why many people think it is better to help a **Learner** have an experience they want *over* someone who is **Pretending** or a **Misguided Person**.

Sometimes, **Pretending** or **Misguided People** may act distressed, as though there was a real emergency, if they don't get their way. You might find them acting like it's not their fault at all when they poorly communicate the difference between an actual emergency and not getting their way, and someone gets hurt because of it. They will probably say something like: "You should have listened."

An example: A **Pretending Person** yelling at you when you are testing your balance on a wooden plank, and then later yelling the same way when you are walking behind a car that starts moving. You might ignore them because you have known them to get distressed about stuff that isn't actually important.

Exercise 1: On another piece of paper, write down the unfilled guidelines of how many of each type of person it's OK to upset if you are a **Learner**:

Everything Knower	64
Self Guider	_____
Wise Leader	_____
Learner	1
Worker	4
Pretending Person	_____
Misguided Person	_____
Bad Guy	256

Answers:

Everything Knower: 64, Self Guider: 16, Wise Leader: 4, Learner: 1, Worker: 4, Pretending Person: 16, Misguided Person: 64, Bad Guy: 256

Becoming a Wise Leader is hard and takes time, but it is worthwhile.

Exercise 2: You are a **Pretending Person**. You and your 13 **Pretending Person** friends are trying to play a game of throwing a football in a field and are complaining about everyone. Three young **Learners** are trying to play a game in that same area and are upsetting your game. You really want to play your game. Here are some options you have:

A. Yell at them to go away.

B. Work on making the field nicer (mowing the grass, painting lines, caring for trees) so they see and go away.

C. Hold a meeting with your friends and start talking about important stuff so the **Learners** don't upset you.

On another piece of paper, fill in the blanks:

1. Which option is the easiest for you? _____

2. Which option would make **Learners** think it's OK to take things from those younger than them? _____

3. Which option will help the **Learners** learn **Worker** skills if they watch? _____

4. Which option will help the **Learners** learn **Wise Leader** skills if they watch? _____

Answers:

1: A, 2: A, 3: B, 4: C

Exercise 3: You are a **Pretending Person** trying to take care of a young group of **Learners**. You *really* want them to pay attention to what you have to say, but they are not. Here are some options you have:

- A: Believe that they are not smart enough to know that you are worth listening to, and try to convince them they are not smart, so they will listen.
- B: Yell really loudly and get angry to frighten them into listening to you.
- C: Try to become a **Wise Leader** and wait until they are comfortable enough to give you another chance to be heard.
- D: Want something else besides having them pay attention to you.

On another piece of paper, fill in the blanks:
1. Which option will take the longest? _____
2. Which option will be the hardest for you? _____
3. Which option will make them doubt themselves? _____
4. Which option will make them scared of you? _____

Answers:
1: C, 2: C, 3: A, 4: B

How Different People Handle Advantages and Disadvantages

Sometimes, through hard work or luck, some people have an advantage compared to others. Sometimes, through laziness or bad luck, other people have a disadvantage compared to others.

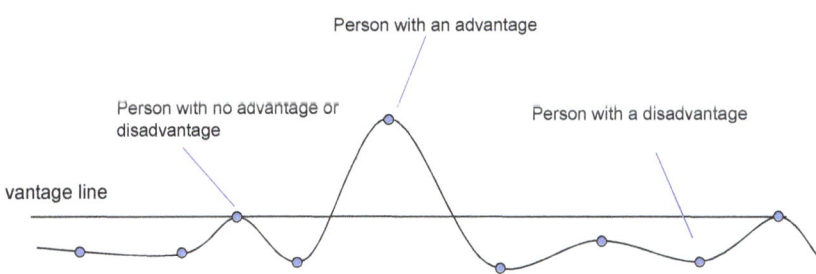

- Being stronger than other people is an advantage.
- Owning more things is an advantage.
- Having a lot of information about how the world works is an advantage.
- Being able to imagine how the world could be better is an advantage.
- Having more close friends is an advantage.
- Being able to let others know what's on your mind is an advantage.
- Being artistic is an advantage.

- Knowing what's going to happen to you and when is an advantage.
- Having control over how other people spend their time is an advantage.
- Anything that gives you extra time in safety without worry is an advantage.

Imagine there is a group of people who live near each other and help each other, but are unable to speak. They have a lot of trouble building things, because, if they work together, they can't tell each other how long a piece of wood should be or how many bricks they need. They can't tell each other what time they need to meet to work on different things.

Workers are having trouble building a house because they can't talk to each other.

One day, the group gains two new members. They have the ability to speak to each other. They can save a lot of time and energy now. They have a great advantage. When they grow up, they will have lots of different options on how to use their advantage.

Way 1: Use Their Advantage to Help the Group

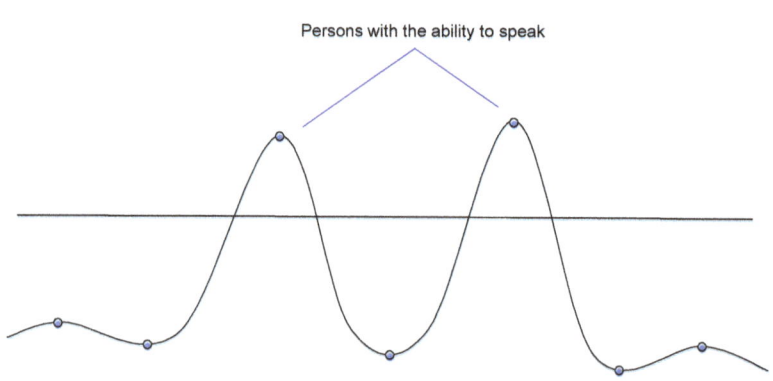

People with the advantage see it as a way to help move your group forward and succeed even more.

The people who can speak can save a lot of time because they can talk about when to meet each other and how many bricks they need. They could even teach other members of the group how to speak. They could speak to each other about emergency procedures and *lead* the group elsewhere, if needed.

Who sees things this way? Definitely **Wise Leaders**. Also, **Everything Knowers**, **Self Guiders**, and some **Learners** and **Workers**.

Wise Leaders have strict rules for themselves when it comes to advantages. They don't accept any advantages they do not deserve. If they have an advantage and it's not their choice, they still try to deserve it and use it to do good. If they could gain an advantage, but it would take time and energy to earn it, they will try to achieve it, and then use it to do good (and will try hard to avoid doing harm while achieving it).

Way 2: View People Who Do Not Have That Advantage as Less Than the People in Your Group

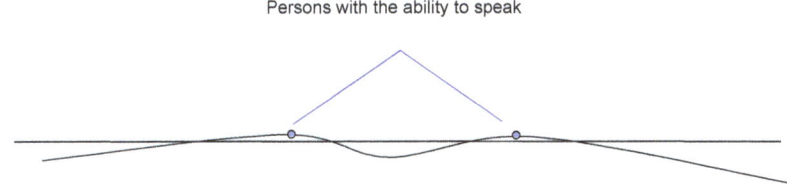

The people with the advantage of having the ability to speak no longer feel like they need to serve the group. They see the other members of the group as less than themselves. If those members without the advantage have sad feelings, it doesn't matter as much as those with the advantage. The advantaged people might even start to think of those members without the advantage as resources for them to use.

Who would do this? **Pretending People**, **Misguided People**, and **Bad Guys** will do this the most. Their brains are very limited on how many people they can treat as equals, which is OK, except that, instead of admitting their limits, they will say that group deserves to be treated poorly. **Learners** and **Workers** might have reasons to use this view too. There may be cases where anyone may use this view. Sometimes people take this view if a bunch of needy people ask them for help all the time. You might have to treat them as if they are less, just for now, because you don't have enough time to talk to everyone.

Examples of people trying out this view: A group of friends calling others who walk by bad names. A king smiling at how hard other people struggle to work and suffer. An adult saying something like, "Those kids go to the candy like vermin go to cheese." (The idea of having to treat children as equals is too hard for them to think about, so they compare them to an animal that most people don't care much about. That way, life is easy for them again.)

A *Learner* realizes one difficulty that those with advantages run into when trying to help others: finding out who to help first.

Sometimes people who see things this way believe that people with a greater advantage should help them.

Those with an even greater advantage might ask themselves:

- Why should I help you if there are people even more disadvantaged than you, who you forgot about?
- What would you do if you had the advantages I have? Would you help the kind of person that you used to be?
- What would happen if you gained an even greater advantage than me? Would you forget about me?

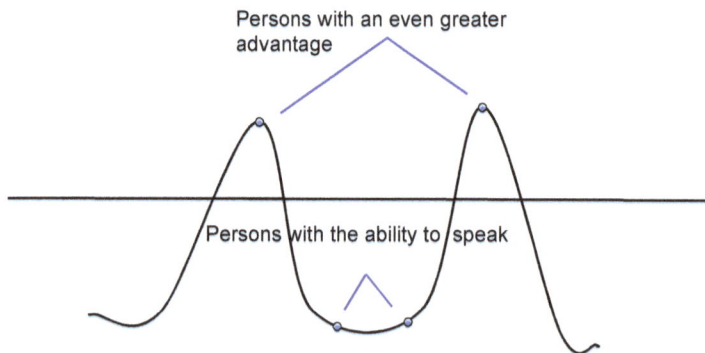

Way 3: See Your Advantage as Not a Real Advantage

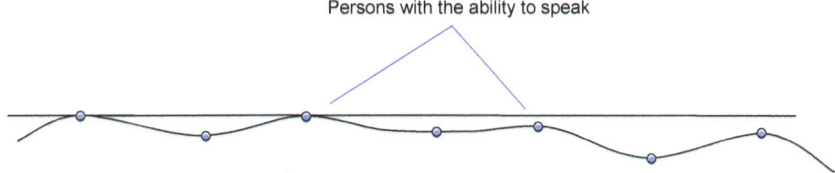

People decide to view their advantage like it's not an advantage at all. Those with the advantage of having the ability to speak will help the rest of the group, but not put too much energy into it. If their advantage gives them more free time, they will spend it having fun or feeling safe, and not trying to improve themselves.

People who hold this view tend to say things like: "I didn't ask for this ability," "I just worry about myself, nothing wrong with that," or "I worked hard for what I got. If they want it, they should work hard too."

Who uses this way? **Workers** would use it the most. **Learners** and **Pretending People** would too.

Way 4: All at Once

A **Self Guider** would be experienced with every one of the above ways at some point, although they would probably make the most use of way 1. There may be some situations where other ways would be appropriate, and they could tell you why. Perhaps even some **Learners** might use their initial advantage to gain an even greater advantage over others, with the intention of switching to helping others later.

Imagine there is a person who really values way 1: "Use their advantage to help the group." Say there is a situation where they have to save two people who have that view. But, in order to save them, they have to take an action following way 2: "See people who do not have that advantage as less than themselves." Should they do that?

Maybe a **Self Guider** would think it's OK.

Testing to See What Kind of Person They Are

Many people do not like to talk about how limited or how selfish they are, and some can't even tell anymore! It would save you a lot of time and help you get along better if they just told you, so you'd know how to treat them. All they need to do is take a little bit of time to let you know.

Unfortunately, that probably will not happen. You might have to take some time away from figuring out how to do good and spend time figuring out what kind of person they are, so you can work out what to do next. It might be especially hard if your way is: "Wait until a person tells you their negative qualities and disadvantages before you treat them like they are not as great as a **Wise Leader**." Many people follow the way of: "It's good to not talk about your negative qualities." Most people will not know how to tell you even if they wanted to! Considering how many of certain types of people there are in the world, it might be better to prepare yourself to figure out if someone has negative qualities *without* them telling you. A **Wise Leader**, who understands this world, will **definitely** see that you will need to test them, and they will be happy to see you do it. They won't even mind if they fail your tests! Yay!

Testing to See If Someone Is an Everything Knower

If they weren't prepared for something that you did, then they are not an Everything Knower.

If they recommend you do something and it doesn't work well for you, and they have trouble realizing that, then you know they are not an Everything Knower.

If something happened that confuses them, then they are not an Everything Knower. Perhaps a Wise Leader, Learner, or Worker.

If they predict something will happen, but it doesn't happen the way they said, they are not an Everything Knower.

Finding Out They Are Not an Everything Knower

Now you know that some of your ways might be just as good for the world as theirs. If you have avoided trying things your way before, you can think about trying them now.

Now you know that you should not fight anyone who opposes their way. (It is recommended that you assume everyone you see is not an Everything Knower.) Also, you have to rethink some ways you checkboxed as good:

- This way is good because an Everything Knower does it, and it will keep our environment working at its best.
- This way is good because an Everything Knower told me.
- This way is good because an Everything Knower acted very angry when I tried a different way, and they would only do that if it was very bad.

Testing to See If Someone Is a Self Guider

Here are a collection of ways to see if someone is a Self Guider:

- If you try really hard to do things their way, and all they tell you is "Good job" or "I'm proud of you," when you expect them to try things your way too, then you know they are not a Self Guider, but a Worker or Pretending Person.
- If you try really hard to impress them by extending their way into other areas of life and they get mad at you, then you know they are not a Self Guider.
- If you try really hard to think about them the way you wish they would think about you, and they seem distracted and unable to pay attention to you long enough to notice, then you know they are not a Self Guider.
- If you have never seen them talk or think about anything related to life and growth since you've known them, they will probably not know how to tell you when it's safe for you to think on your own. You know they are not a Self Guider. Maybe they are a Worker or a Pretending Person.
- If you ask them why they do something, and they tell you that it's because everyone else does it, then they are not a Self Guider.
    - o If they seem unwilling or embarrassed to share the reasons they do things, then they might be a

Pretending Person or a **Worker**.
- If they do share the reasons, but the reasons are more disappointing than you expected, and the action seems unlikely to make a more thriving environment, then they might be a **Worker**.

- If they do something the same way everyone else does and they don't like it, and do not plan on changing it, then they are not a **Self Guider**.

- If they do something the same way everyone else does and they don't like it but pretend to like it, then they are not a **Self Guider** – maybe a **Pretending Person**.

- If you try a new way, and it's easy to see that it makes a more thriving environment than their way, and they are not interested in this new way at all, then they are probably not a **Self Guider**.

*A **Learner** invented the "Double Hammer" for hammering 2 nails in at once. Their caretaker doesn't really care.*

- If you try really hard to think how they want you to think, and only try to do good, but they still blame you for things that go wrong, then you know they are not a **Self Guider**. Perhaps a **Pretending Person**.

- If you are new to the world and they admit they do not **know everything**, and they *don't* treat you like you are dumb when they explain it to you, then they might be a **Self Guider**!

Finding Out They Are a **Self Guider**

If you find out they are a **Self Guider**, now you have a very heavy responsibility on your shoulders. Many people in this world wish to have the experience of growing up with and learning from a **Self Guider**. After you learn what you can from them, others will want to know what you know. They may try to communicate it in unconventional ways. You know their goal is to do good in the world, so it's your responsibility to try to work out what they require of you, to help them achieve their potential or undo any harm they might have caused.

Finding Out They Are Not a Self Guider

If you find out they are not a **Self Guider**, they will probably never tell you when it's safe for you to think and decide things for yourself. You must decide on your own when you are ready (if you find out they are a **Pretending Person**, or worse, then you may be better off thinking for yourself right away!).

You now know it's **not OK** to try to spread their ways to other people. It's **not OK** to put all your energy into imagining how the world would work if everyone did things according to one of their ways. It's also **not OK** to put a lot of extra thought into what their words mean, especially if their words are negative.

(It is recommended that you should assume that everyone you see is **not** a **Self Guider**.)

Now you know that if someone doesn't bother explaining something to you, it's not because they don't think you are a good enough person to deserve an explanation, but because they are *not* smart enough to know how to explain it! They are probably not able to tell you some things about the world and why they do things a particular way because they don't know how to explain it – or they don't even remember!

Sometimes **Learners** try experimenting with having the negative qualities of their caretakers for a couple of reasons:

1. They try to understand what their caretakers are dealing with and what they are thinking.
2. They try to see things from the perspective of people who have that disadvantage, in order to know how to work with them better.
3. They try to let their caretakers know that they are still greater, and they are free to improve themselves.

If you know someone is not a **Self Guider**, you now know it's NOT OK to take on their limitations and negative qualities in order to communicate concepts like these with them. If you do it to let them know it's OK to treat you differently, in addition to not knowing how you wish to be treated, they probably won't know why you have you taken their negative qualities, and they might not even *realize* you have taken their negative qualities! (Most caretakers don't pay that close attention.)

Remember, you may want to rethink some ways you checkboxed as good:

- This way is good because a **Self Guider** does it and they can account for everything they do.
- This way is good because it will help me impress a **Self Guider** enough that they will explain more of this world to me, so I can better figure out how to do the most good.
- This way is good because a **Self Guider** does it, and it shows them I believe in them, so they will tell me how they discovered that it's good.
- This way is good because if I do it enough, they will understand that the effects of their ways are actually bad and try things my way.
- This way is good for now, because it will help a **Self Guider** figure out that it's actually bad, so they then become an **Everything Knower**, and then the world will be even better.

These are all ones that you might want to rethink!

Testing to See If Someone Is a **Wise Leader**

See how **Pocobian** they are by communicating in unconventional ways:

> **Pocobian:** A quality of a person who thinks very hard about the **p**ers**o**n **o**ne **co**uld **b**e. They are someone who asks themselves, "If I were being taken care of, could I think of any messages so important, that it would be worthwhile upsetting the person I am now for just a chance to communicate it?" and tends to come up with good answers. They use these answers to further guide their actions.
>
> If you have used up all the words you can think of to try to communicate with them that something is discouraging you, or would create a bad future if it continued, you can treat someone as if they are very **Pocobian**. If someone isn't good at thinking of good answers, you know they are not a **Wise Leader**. A **Learner** could imagine there could be an answer, but currently needs to think about themselves, so that they may become a **Wise Leader** someday. **Workers** are not very good

at thinking about that kind of stuff. A **Pretending Person** might do some very unexpected things, like being very confident that you want to be bad and therefore be treated like a bad person.

* Since there are so few **Wise Leaders** in the world, you should only use this test if you have a plan of what to do if they fail the test as poorly as a **Pretending Person** would. You should never trust anyone to pass this test without a backup plan! A real **Wise Leader**, **Self Guider**, or **Everything Knower** would *not* be disappointed in you if you didn't trust them. They would be happy that you are so willing to do good that you put some thought into what to do if they let you down!

Here are some more ways to work out if someone is a **Wise Leader**:

- A **Wise Leader** would realize they are responsible for however you treat them. Here's a test: Try to impress them by treating them as they treated you. If they don't like it, then you know they aren't **Wise Leaders**. In that case, you may have discovered a **Pretending Person** or a **Worker**.

- When it comes to those who lead others, you might hear them complain about how difficult being in charge is. They blame the people they're in charge of for being wrong or broken, before they wonder what they could do to improve themselves. They might be heard saying how real **Wise Leaders** are lucky their subjects behave so well, without wondering what they themselves are doing wrong. They're definitely not **Wise Leaders**. Probably just a **Pretending Person**.

- If there is an unfortunate incident in which you know you are innocent, you can figure out what kind of person you are dealing with by acting sorry anyway. If they still try to figure out what happened, then they may be **Wise Leader**. If they decide to punish you without trying to figure out what happened, then you know they might be a **Worker** or a **Pretending Person**.

- If they don't understand something that you are making progress in, but try to stop you anyway, then they are not a **Wise Leader**.

- If they accept a lot of the credit for something you succeeded in by yourself, then you know they are not a **Wise Leader**. They could be a **Learner** or **Worker** who thinks the person giving credit is an **Everything Knower** (they are thinking, "Since they gave me credit, it must be true"). They could also be a **Pretending Person** who thinks they deserve as much credit as possible.

- If they can't tell you why they do everything they do when you ask them, and they are sorry about it, then they might be a **Wise Leader**.

- If you demonstrate how committed you are to them and their cause to do good, a **Wise Leader** will see it and try to find a way to tell you that they aren't actually that great.

- If they don't like it when they see you pretend to be happy around them, they might be a **Wise Leader**.

- If they want you to tell them when you would prefer to be left alone, they might be a **Wise Leader**.

- If you see them use their advantages to help others, then they might be a **Wise Leader**.

Finding Out They Are a Wise Leader

Now you know it's OK to do things that will impress them because it will help build a better future for everyone.

Finding Out They Are Not a Wise Leader

Now you know they may not remember how they treated you or what effect it has on you. They might not realize it was a mistake. You should plan what you do next, considering they might not remember or say they are sorry. They may not tell their **Wise Leader** friends what mistake they discovered, in order to keep others from experiencing the same damage they gave you.

Now you know that they might not use their advantages for good. You should not expect them to use their advantages to help others without those advantages. You now know it's not OK to put a lot of energy into giving them more advantages. If something makes them happy and you don't see how it would help them do good, then it's not worth the energy spent in trying to get it to them.

Additionally, now you know that no matter how many things you eliminate from the world that upset them, they probably won't use their extra time not being upset to see things your way, play with you, help others, or improve themselves. They will probably just find more things to get upset about! Now you also know that eliminating things that upset them might not even be good for the world.

Now you know they may not be smart enough to realize that they don't know you very well. They probably won't give you good advice on what to do with your time. If you suspect some of their advice may *not* help you develop into someone better able to do good, you might be right.

Remember, you may want to rethink some ways you checkboxed as good:

- Doing things this way is good because a **Wise Leader** acted confidently when they did things this way.
- Doing things this way is good because a **Wise Leader** copied it from someone else they trust as a **Wise Leader**.

Testing to See If Someone Is a **Worker**

See if they have **Waylock:**

People with **waylock** are not able to change how they feel about something, even if they have good reasons. They won't even try things a different *way* just to see how it goes.

- If you see them struggling to try to feel a different way about something (like fear of heights) and they are unable to, then you know they may be closer to a **Worker** or a **Pretending Person**.
- If you see them understanding that there are good reasons to change how they feel, but they stay the same, then you know they may be a **Worker** or a **Pretending Person**.
- If they are unwilling to feel a different way about something just to try and see how it goes, then you know they may be a **Worker** or a **Pretending Person**.
- If they are sad about having **Waylock**, they might be a **Worker**.
- If they come up with strange and complicated excuses to get out of thinking about things a different way, then they probably have **Waylock** and might be a **Pretending Person** or a **Worker**.

Here are some more ways to see if someone is a **Worker**:

- If their days are mostly **work**, **fun**, and **rest**, they might be a **Worker**.
- If you would have to get good at things that **don't** help you make the world a more thriving place, in order to spend quality time with them, then they might be a **Worker**.

- You can try things their way to see if the outcomes are good or bad. If you try to demonstrate that an outcome is bad, a **Worker** won't be interested in knowing, or they won't understand what you're trying to show them.

- If you have never heard them use words of any kind to describe their negative qualities when talking to others, then they might be a **Worker**.

- If they seem very happy and content to talk about very small scale things with their friends, then they might be a **Worker**.

- If you notice their meaning of "be good" is a little different from yours. Yours is something like, "Live up to your potential to be independent and knowledgeable enough to be helpful to the world." If theirs is something like, "Take care of objects, make sure things look nice, and don't do things that upset me," then they might be a **Worker** or **Pretending Person**.

- If they don't feel responsible for the effect their ways would have on the world around them if lots of people do things that way, then they might be a **Worker**.

- If they do things that they cannot explain easily and don't know where they came from, then they might be a **Worker**.

Finding Out They Are a Worker

Now you know that lots of things they say and do aren't very carefully thought through or planned ahead of time.

Now you know it's OK to do things that would impress someone else.

Now you know you can't trust them to respond well to all your actions. Now you will have to think about what to do or say if they respond poorly to something you bring up.

Now you know it's OK to defy the **Worker's** way and not treat others how a **Worker** treated you when you used to believe in them.

Now you know it's OK to think only a little bit about their advice or words.

Don't expect them to be willing to take turns trying other ways. They would not feel in your debt if you helped them see the effect of their ways on yourself. Their ways may not be their own, so they don't care.

Finding Out They Are Not a Worker, But a Pretending Person, Misguided Person, or Bad Guy

Now you know that their ability to figure out how much control they should have over what other people do with their time has been damaged. They may continue to try to have more and more control over other people's time. Nothing inside them can tell them to stop. They must rely on others to convince them to stop. They might have a very hard time realizing how much suffering and damage they have the potential to cause.

Testing to See If Someone Is a Pretending Person

If they:

- Make fun of you for not knowing things that there is no way you could have known about.
- Get upset when you don't know things that there is no way you could have known about.
- Gain a lot of enjoyment from seeing you fail.
- Are happy to see you suffer how they once suffered.
- Get mad at you for not automatically knowing about their weaknesses or negative qualities, and being able to work around them.
- Treat you like you are not smart if you don't know about their negative qualities.
- Accepting, and believing they deserve, the respect of an Everything Knower, without being one.
- Are good at remembering and recalling moments when you weren't at your best.
- Think they know exactly how you feel, what you are, and what you like.
- Tell you that you didn't try your best to be good, when you did.
- Get mad at you (instead of themselves) when they fail your Wise Leader tests.
- Are unprepared for the things you do when you are young and predictable (like if they put a bucket of gold in the middle of the room when you are a baby, and are surprised if you knock it over).

A Caretaker places a bucket of gold next to a Baby Learner and gets very surprised when the baby knocks it over, proving themself to be more of a Pretending Person.

You can be more and more sure that this person is a **Pretending Person**.

If they are very uncomfortable when you act like a **Learner** sometimes acts to communicate they are still a **Learner**, you can be even more sure they are a **Pretending Person**. Examples include: being confused when you are working with something you aren't familiar with, like a lock or a wrench, or being very hesitant when entering a new situation, like going into a room full of strangers.

You can pretend to be fearful or worried about being a person with qualities you don't want. You can act like you are worried about being uninteresting, boring, not smart, unable to help the world be better, or unpleasant to be around. A **Pretending Person** or **Misguided Person** will pick up on your worry and try to treat you like that anyway, even if they don't know you well.

You can do something that you know is wrong (but you intend to fix once you are more capable) just to hear from them why it is wrong. If they say you are bad after you do it and are unable to explain why, you know they might be a **Pretending Person**. If they can explain why and give you guidance on how to correct it, they might be a **Self Guider**. (You should not trust most people to know what to do or say when you do something wrong on purpose, so only use this test if you have to.)

Finding Out They Are a **Pretending Person**

Now you know you should not use their ways on most people (especially large groups of people). You should not talk with the leaders of groups of people the same way a **Pretending Person** talks with you. You should not expect good leaders to act like them.

Now you know you should not copy how they feel in many situations. They might get mad at the world when something goes wrong when, if they thought about it hard enough, they might realize was their fault.

Now you know they may never feel bad about how they responded to an action. They might believe it was right for the rest of their life.

Now you know it's OK to try ways that are opposite to theirs. But which ways are good and worth keeping, and which ways are bad and worth doing the opposite? (And which ways should you still support or go against, but not so strongly?) You could try to pay attention to what type of advice they give you and *categorize* it that way. If you divide their advice into "Advice for the Mind" and "Advice for the Body," for example, you might notice that the advice they give you for the body is usually correct and the advice for the mind is usually incorrect. (Currently, in this world, it's more well known what is beneficial for the *body*. In terms of the *mind*, however, there are still many unknowns. Even one person's mind might work differently from another!)

Good Advice for the Body	Possibly Bad Advice for the Mind?
Brush your teeth	Sit still and be quiet for hours
Get shots so you don't get sick	Get good at a skill before you feel ready
Eat vegetables	Keep on doing worksheets even if your mind is tired

You might need to be alone when you are learning new skills. They probably follow the way of, "If someone does something that doesn't work, it's proof they are not smart," so they will make fun of you for making a mistake. You will need to make mistakes in order to get more skilled at something. They will continue to treat you like you are unskilled if they watch you practice.

Now you know you can't trust them in certain ways. They might have a very simplified view of how *you* think about things. They might not think you can handle certain concepts, and they think that, since they know the proper way to do things, you do not need to understand how it could work in different ways. To be a **Wise Leader** someday, you need to understand as much as possible. Unfortunately, you might have to take time away from figuring out how to do the most good, and spend some time figuring out what information you can share with a **Pretending Person** and what you cannot. Example: If you played with something harmless at school, but the **Pretending Person** thought it was bad, they might punish you if you told them.

There may have been a point in their life where they were asking for help in some way, but didn't get it, so they gave up. They might try some very unconventional ways to ask for help now. They will probably do things to try to prevent you from helping them, or do things to you that hurt your ability to help them. It may be the case that the more they hurt you, the more help they may need. You might not have learned enough to be able to help them yet, so you might have to forget about that **Pretending Person** for now and move on.

Testing to See If Someone Is a Misguided Person

If they:

- Aren't very happy and welcoming to people new to this world.
- Act like it's good to give people a very hard time if they are new to this world.
- Force you to change your ways by putting you in a room alone with them, or stare at you, waiting until you do something they want.
- Force you to change by hitting you until you stop doing something that seems good.
- Shout at you really loudly, asking why you do things that you believe a **Learner** would do to become a **Wise Leader** someday.
- Say their family deserves more than others as the reason for taking things from others.
- Say other people are "dumb" or "stupid" for trusting others (like calling a child dumb for leaving a toy on their lawn where it could get stolen, or calling someone dumb for hoping to marry someone they could trust).
- Are not very nice to **Workers** who just want to help them.
- Lie about how the world works, so you do what they want (example: saying that someone who could be a **Wise Leader** will get mad if you don't stop playing, but in reality it's the **Misguided Person** who is annoyed when you play).

- Lie about how *you* work, so you do what they want (example: saying you're allergic to mud so you can't play in it, when actually, they just don't want to clean up mud).
- Force you to smile when you try one of their non-working ways, even though they know you are not happy on the inside.

You can be more and more sure they are a **Misguided Person**.

Finding Out They Are a Misguided Person

Now you know it would take a great deal more effort to help them than it would to get along with new friends and help the needy. They may even be beyond helping.

Now you know they will try to change you into someone you don't want to be. You will have to take effort away from being a better person to resist them.

Now you know that you may have to rethink most of the ways they have given you, if you want to get along with different types of people.

Testing to See If Someone Is a Bad Guy

How to tell if someone is a **Bad Guy**

- If you would have to do bad things to get along with them, like hurting, stealing, or saying you'll hurt someone, then they might be a **Bad Guy**.
- If you always have to worry about what they will do next, they might be a **Bad Guy**.
- If they decide who you should hate, they might be a **Bad Guy**.
- If they tell you to get revenge on people you don't know, they might be a **Bad Guy**.
- If they keep you from seeing the outside world, they might be a **Bad Guy**.
- If they say some children deserve to be hurt because their parents were bad, they might be a **Bad Guy**.
- If they hurt people who aren't **Bad Guys** and are just trying

to live their lives, they might be a **Bad Guy**.

Finding Out They Are a Bad Guy

Do you live in a place where **Bad Guys** are considered bad, or are they considered normal?

If they are considered bad, then you could report to most people around you that a **Bad Guy** is hurting you or plans to hurt someone, and they will come to your aid.

If **Bad Guys** are considered normal, however, you might have to find a way to move to a place where people will support you in your tough situation.

Getting Along With People

Reasons to Do or Not Do Something

Being Naturally Impelled

When a normal person's body, mind, nature, or their instinct really *really* wants them to do something, it will make it so they feel really bad, in pain, or not feel like themselves until they do it. They do it because **nature impelled** them.

If someone does something because nature impelled them, it usually helps their goals in two ways:

1. They are naturally drawn towards the right environment for achieving their goals.
2. Being in that type of environment tells their brain and body to work well without problems.

Doing something because you are naturally impelled is a very good reason to do something if you don't know much about the world yet. Doing so should *usually* make a **Self Guider** happy if they were your caretaker.

Exercise: Match what nature impels you to do with the very good reason it helps you reach your goals. Write down which number goes with which letter on another piece of paper.

How It Helps Your Body and Brain Work Well Without Problems	How It Helps Your Goals
1. I'm eating because I'm hungry.	A. I need oxygen to live.
2. I'm going to the bathroom because my bladder hurts.	B. I need nutrients to live.
3. I need to swim up because I panic when I can't breathe.	C. If I get too injured, I can't help out.
4. I need to stop standing on this hot metal because it hurts.	D. I need to flush out the water in me to make room for new water.

Being **lonely** is a common reason people are naturally impelled to do something.

1. Working together with other people on a goal helps it get done faster.
2. Being around other people lets their brain think well and their body work well.

If someone has a goal but is alone, the task becomes harder because:

1. They have to do everything by themselves.
2. Their brain tells them not to think as well and their body not to work as well because they are alone.

This means they could decide to work on a goal a friend is working on (even if they don't think the goal is for the best) because it would be easier than trying to get themselves to work on a different goal alone.

People in extreme situations sometimes decide to not do something they are naturally impelled to because it hurts their goals to do good.

Exercise: Match what naturally impels you to take an action with how it could hurt your goals. Write down what number goes to what letter on another piece of paper.

How It Helps Your Body and Brain Work Well Without Problems	How It Could Hurt Your Goals
1. I want to eat because I'm hungry.	A. I don't want food because I want to share it with my friend who is even hungrier.
2. I want to go to the bathroom because my bladder hurts.	B. I'm a lifeguard and I have to dive down to rescue someone before I can get oxygen.
3. I need to swim up because I panic when I can't breathe.	C. I'll have to hold it in to get my friend to the hospital first.
4. All I can think about is getting off this hot metal when I walk on it.	D. I will have to walk in pain to get to the exit because there is a fire.

Answers:
1.B; 2.D; 3.A; 4.C

Answers:
1.A; 2.C; 3.B; 4.D

There might be some situations where it would be best to be lonely too. If you work alone and it's not your choice, or there is a situation where working alone could help more people than working together, then being naturally impelled hurts you more than it helps. Example: if you live in a place where you only know Misguided People, then you might have to be alone to make the world better.

For Self Guiders, they never *ever* do things because they are naturally impelled. They found a way to do things without pain, panic, hunger, or loneliness affecting them. It's a very good **advantage**.

Being Impelled by Others

Sometimes, people who have control of other people's time see that being naturally impelled works so well for getting people to do things, that they will invent their own ways to impel people to do what they want (sometimes called a **punishment**). If the person does what they want to avoid punishment, that person is being impelled by another.

Examples of people trying to make other people do things:

- Yelling at someone when they are exploring a dangerous area (getting yelled at makes them uncomfortable, and they want the discomfort to go away, so they leave the area).
- Pinching someone who is accidentally stepping on your foot.
- Putting someone in jail for hurting others.
- Hitting a kid with a ruler for not paying attention.

Imagine you had to get some information to your caretaker that would help them do good, but it is hard or impossible for you to say to them at the moment. You might try to communicate it by impelling the other person. These are called **Unconventional Ways To Communicate.** If someone had the energy or the knowledge to tell you something, they would say "Ouch" if you stepped on their foot, and then you would know to stop. But what if someone didn't know what to say, or couldn't? If not, they might pinch you to

let you know. Someone getting pinched is certainly better for the world than someone having a broken foot!

A Self Guider is happy that the Learner tried to impel him to stop backing up by pinching him so the Learner wouldn't fall off a cliff. The Self Guider knows Learners sometimes can't think of what to say.

Sometimes, people use unconventional ways to communicate to tell someone that their ways are hurting them or their dear ones, or could hurt them in the future. They hope that it will cause them to rethink their ways. Things get out of hand when people broaden their use of unconventional ways to communicate with people other than the person causing them harm. Since there aren't any **Self Guiders** or **Everything Knowers** in the world, it is extremely difficult to find out what really happened and how to help them.

Exercise: On another piece of paper, mark the Unconventional Way to Communicate whose message isn't meant for a **Learner** like you, but for someone else.

1. Someone yells at you when you keep waving a spoonful of peanut butter in front of someone who is allergic to peanuts.

2. You find a dollar in front of a house and knock on the door to see if it's theirs. Someone yells, "I told you, I don't have it! Now leave me alone!"

3. You see a sign outside someone's house that says, "Due to recent robberies, there is a vicious dog that will attack anyone on sight!"

4. Someone is walking down the street waving their hat in front of your face, in a place where hats are against the rules.

Answers.
1. Meant for you
2. Not meant for you
3. Not meant for you
4. Not meant for you

If you are a leader, trying to make a **Self Guider** do something by impelling them won't work. A **Self Guider** will always do something about it. They might first try to find out if there is a good reason they should do things that way, and then tell you how to say it. If that doesn't work, they might go along with it until you figure out that it's wrong for yourself. If that doesn't work, they may try to resolve it with words and actions. If that also doesn't work, they may even use force. Unlike **Workers**, **Self Guiders** **would never accept people making them do something as just the way the world is**. They are so good and can communicate so well, it's best that you just tell them why. They are either understanding why, fighting it, or planning on fighting it in the future. It's never a waste of time to convince a **Self Guider** that a way they support is wrong. They would want to know. If you convince them, they will **defy** this way and defy whatever *naturally impels* them, or whoever *forcefully impels* them to support that way, right alongside you!

Exercise: On another piece of paper, **put an X** on the reason a **Misguided Person** wouldn't want to do something. **Put a check** next to the reason a **Self Guider** wouldn't want to do something.

1. Hurting someone and taking their money.	A. "They have the potential to do a lot of good and to make the world a better place. I want them to live healthily and not be afraid."	B. "If they notice I'm trying to hurt them, they might start fighting me and hurting me."
2. Pushing everyone out of the way when you are walking.	A. "If I push people, they might get mad and push me back."	B. "If I push people, they might fall, and it will hurt their goals."

3. Taking someone's toy they are playing with.	A. "If I don't let this person finish experiencing it until they are done, it might keep them from becoming a **Wise Leader** who could help the world a lot someday. Everyone should get a chance to be a **Wise Leader**!"	B. "If I take this toy, the teacher will take it from me anyway."
4. Following someone who wants to get away from you.	A. "I don't want to follow this person because they think being alone would be for the best. Maybe they are tired and have reached their limit for being around people, and need to rest for next time."	B. "I don't want to follow this person because they will get mad and call me names."
5. Disobeying orders from your commander to take food from children to feed your army.	A. "I am kind of hungry and If I don't follow orders, my commander could yell and punish me. I had better take the food."	B. "I'm not going to take food from those kids. My commander can yell at me and try to punish me all he wants, but it will never work on me. If he tries to take from those kids, I'll have to stop him."

Answers:

1. A.✓ B.✗
2. A.✗ B.✓
3. A.✓ B.✗
4. A.✓ B.✗
5. A.✗ B.✓

Would a **Self Guider** try to make other people do things? They certainly would not try to impel other **Self Guiders**, but it is unknown when a **Self Guider** would think it's OK to make someone else do something.

Wise Leaders, **Learners**, and **Workers** could honestly tell you if they did or didn't do something because someone was impelling them. They would say something like, "I'm doing it because my boss is forcing me to." Everyone above them (**Self Guiders** and

Everything Knowers) would not do something for that reason. Everyone below them (**Pretending People**, **Misguided People**, and **Bad Guys**) usually wouldn't know how to say it and would try not to think about it or pretend they wanted to do that all along. If they do tell you, they might treat you like you are not smart because you didn't know that.

The Right Setting Test

If a caretaker is **impelling** you to stop doing something, you can **test** what kind of person they are by saying something like this: "Caretaker, instead of yelling, taking away my toys, or hurting me, would you just tell me the reason I shouldn't run around without clothes? If you don't think it's the **right setting** now, would you tell me when it would be the **right setting**?" Different types of people might respond differently:

- "Are you stupid?" or "Now you are just trying to be a brat!" is something a **Misguided Person** might say.

- "Never," or "When I say so," is something a **Pretending Person** would say (**Pretending People** aren't very good at imagining exceptions to rules).

- A **Worker** will hope you do not ask questions like these because talking or thinking about this sort of topic makes them uncomfortable. They don't know what to say.

- A **Worker** or **Learner** might say the name of someone with control over what they do with their time. Perhaps this person could answer your question.

- "Oh, I never thought about that before," is likely to be said by a **Worker** or a **Wise Leader**. "In the bathtub, when you're alone only. You shouldn't show other people your private parts," is something a **Worker** or a **Wise Leader** in a hurry might say.

- A **Wise Leader** who is on the path to becoming a **Self Guider** might say, "One of the reasons people get upset when they see you without clothes is because it further keeps **Bad Guys** from being able to see all the good you could do for the world, and instead, makes them care about hurting you *even less*. People who see you without clothes are upset because they worry that they can't stop the **Bad Guys**. They can, however, stop you from taking off your clothes. So, if we change things so the world is without **Bad Guys**, then it would be the **right setting**. Another reason may be because the people around you have **waylock**, and are unable to change how upset they feel when they see a child run around without clothes. It may be seen as best to upset the child running around without clothes than to upset the people who see them. In fact, they may have ways to **impel** someone's caretaker to stop their child from running around without clothes. Like sending their caretaker to jail. If we change it so people stopped trying to **impel** me to **impel** you to keep your clothes on, that would be another **right setting**. Another **right setting** could be to live with a group of people who all don't want to wear clothes. Another **right setting** is if your clothes were on fire, or there was some other kind of emergency."

- A true Self Guider might say, "You are right; now is the **right setting** for you to run around without clothes!" and then they would 1. stop all the **Bad Guys**, 2. let the people with **waylock** be upset and, 3. stop all the people who try to put them in jail for letting you take off your clothes.

Being Limited

Sometimes when someone tells you, "If you do that, I will do something not very good," there could be two other reasons for that in addition to wanting to impel you: **Limits** and **For-the-best Limits**.

Limits are things that a person is unable to do even if they want to.

Limits are things like:

- "If you hit me, I will fall and not play with you."
- "If you make me study really hard all day every day, I will not talk to your friends well."

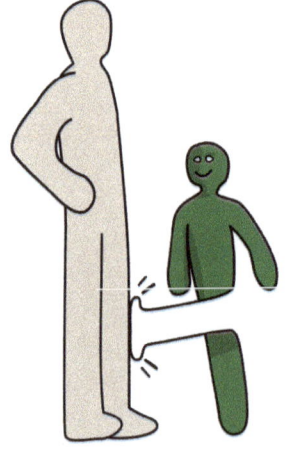

This Everything Knower is invincible, so it's okay to kick them.

If you try hitting a person who is invincible, and they say, "I will stop playing with you if you keep on doing that," they are trying to impel you not to hit them. Since there aren't any people who are invincible, they actually cannot play with you because they are in pain and maybe even can't move their body, because it doesn't work anymore – they have reached their limit.

If someone tells you they will not talk to your friends well, after you make them study all day, *and* they are ready for anything, then they are trying to impel you to let them stop studying. However, since they probably are not ready for everything, it is likely to be a limit. Most people cannot shift tasks so quickly after working on one for so long. They are limited.

Exercise: On another piece of paper, **put a check** next to the view that sees the situation as a **limit** of the person, and **put an X** next to the view that sees the situation as someone trying to **impel** the other.

Situations	View A	View B
1. "If you keep on making loud noises, I will not get ice cream from the ice cream truck."	A. Loud noises hurt their ears and they will not be able to hear the ice cream truck if it goes by.	B. They have invincible ears that do not hurt. They are just not getting you ice cream because they are mean.
2. "If you keep hitting the stove, I will not make you dinner."	A. The stove is unbreakable, and they are just saying that because they are mean.	B. If you keep on hitting the stove, it will break. They need the stove to make dinner.
3. "If you keep on breaking other people's things, I won't take care of you as well."	A. They are just trying to get you to stop breaking people's things, and saying this is a way to get you to stop.	B. When you break other people's things, they have to pay for them. If they run out of money, they will have to get another job to get more. If they are working and not at home, they can't take care of you very well.

Answers:

1. A. ✓ B. X
2. A. X B. ✓
3. A. X B. ✓

67

This Misguided Person is angry and confused about how his chair can't be used as a toothbrush.

How a **Self Guider** might answer some questions from a **Misguided Person** about limits:

Misguided Person: "Whenever I try to use this chair as a toothbrush, it doesn't work. What's wrong with it? Even yelling at it doesn't help."

Self Guider: "Chairs are limited in many ways and are not made to be used as toothbrushes."

Misguided Person: "Whenever I try to play a **new** game on an **old** computer, it doesn't work. What's wrong with it?"

Self Guider: "You might be expecting too much out of it. You could either play old games on your old computer or buy a new computer to play new games."

Misguided Person: "Whenever I do extreme stunts off of ramps with my car, the Check Engine light on my car keeps flashing and annoys me. What's wrong with it?"

Self Guider: "It's limited to normal everyday use. It wasn't made to do extreme stunts for long, and when it warns you that it could break soon, it might actually be telling the truth that it has reached its limit. It's telling you to **help you** get the best use out of your car."

Misguided Person: "Whenever I give someone some work that I think they could do, they cannot. Even when I ask them: 'What's wrong with you?' it doesn't help."

Self Guider: "People come in all different shapes and sizes. Their minds also work in different ways. Some reach their limits faster than others. This person might have reached their limit. There are three things you can do with people who reach their limits like that:

1. Kill them so they cannot let their limit harm those around them.

2. Move people with that limit to a different group where they can live in peace and not bother anyone else.
3. Let them live in our part of the world and help them find jobs where their limits do not hold them back.

The world we live in now was built on valuing option 3, above all others. I have seen some groups of people that used option 1 and some that used option 2, but they didn't work out too well. Many now consider people who use option 1 **Bad Guys**, and would try to stop them with force if they used that way on others."

For-the-best Limits

For-the-best Limits are things someone can't do because they are trying to be a good person and can see that it's not for the best.

For-the-best Limits are things like:

1. "I could make my only job in life to be putting toothpaste on your toothbrush, but I will not do that because it's not for the best."
2. "I could do nothing but wait for you to return home from work, but I will not because it's not for the best."

Sometimes, you might think someone wants you to do something that isn't for the best, but they think it is. In the wild, male lions sit around all day and don't do anything, and female lions get the food. But, with the male lions being well rested all the time, they can act and help if there is an emergency. Since there are lots of dangers and emergencies in the wild, it might be for the best.

Since it's impossible for people who aren't **Everything Knowers** to know someone's **intent**, it will be hard to tell if they are being lazy, or actually have a very good plan in mind. Maybe it will be a good idea to not be too mad if you must say "No" when they ask you to do something that seems not for the best.

Exercise: On another piece of paper, write down the reason someone would say <u>no</u> if you asked them to do the following:

1. You are now old enough to dive off the very high diving board. Can you grab my goggles I left up there and jump down? "No."

- Impelled by nature
- Impelled by another
- Limit
- For-the-best Limit

2. Could you ask the mean teacher how to spell a naughty word for me, please? "No."
- Impelled by nature
- Impelled by another
- Limit
- For-the-best Limit

3. Could you jump up into space and kick down the moon for me, please? "No."
- Impelled by nature
- Impelled by another
- Limit
- For-the-best Limit

4. Could you stop learning about being a good person and get me a drink from the fridge and make me a sandwich? I'm very busy watching this game show. "No."
- Impelled by nature
- Impelled by another
- Limit
- For-the-best Limit

5. Could you go to a store 100 miles away and get me a toy? "No."
- Impelled by nature
- Impelled by another
- Limit
- For-the-best Limit

6. Could you stay with me for a million years? "No."
- Impelled by nature
- Impelled by another
- Limit
- For-the-best Limit

7. Could you read the newspaper while I'm making a lot of noise banging on pots and pans? "No,"
- Impelled by nature
- Impelled by another
- Limit
- For-the-best Limit

8. Could you skip doing your taxes this year and play with me instead? "No."
   - Impelled by nature
   - Impelled by another
   - Limit
   - For-the-best Limit

Possible Answers:

1. Impelled by nature
2. Impelled by another
3. Limit
4. For-the-best Limit
5. For-the-best Limit
6. Limit
7. Impelled by nature
8. Impelled by another

Answer explanations:

These questions could have different answers, depending on how you think about them. Here are the explanations for the answers given:

1. Here, even though it's OK for them to go up the diving board, the thing that would prevent a younger person from jumping is fear, which comes from the inside, so they are being impelled by nature.

2. Mean teachers have punishments for kids who say naughty words. If they ask a mean teacher to spell a naughty word, they might have to say the word to the teacher. Since this teacher might yell at them if they say a naughty word, they don't want to ask. The child would then be impelled by another not to ask.

3. Since normal people can't jump up and kick down the moon, it's a Limit.

4. Since it's possible for them to make a sandwich for their caretaker, it's not a limit. Someone learning to be a good person is better for the world than someone watching a game show. They are meant for better things than getting drinks and making sandwiches. The answer is For-the-best Limit.

5. It's possible to travel 100 miles to get a toy if you have a car (or even without), but it's probably not the best use of a

71

person's time. The answer could be For-the-best Limit.

6. Normal people don't live for a million years, so they can't stay with someone for a million years. The answer is Limit.

7. Something inside of them would tell them not to read well if there are loud noises like the banging of pots and pans. The answer could be that they were impelled by nature.

8. If someone didn't do their taxes, they could be arrested by the government and have to go to jail. So the answer may be that they are impelled by another. There might be different answers, depending on how you think about it, though. Maybe they want to pay their taxes instead of playing with the child because they know it's for the best.

Care Control Reasons

Sometimes, people who have control over what you do with your time stop you from doing something that you like. *However*, the only reason you like it is because it might help you to be a good person someday. It is a case of being impelled by another, but instead of doing something that hurts you, it hurts your goals to help others. The person you really like who's in control of your time, therefore, hurts their own ability to be helped by you. They make a **Care Control Reason** for you to do what they want. They sometimes make you wonder, "If I were a better person or if I didn't exist at all, would my dear ones be better off?"

Examples:

- "If you keep on accidentally tripping, I will have to take away your telescope."
- "If you don't look up at the board, I will take away your crayons that you are using to draw a picture for me."
- "I'm stopping you from pretending to play doctor to help me when I get older because you didn't finish your food."
- "If you don't move rocks faster, I will get mad and hurt you. Now that you are hurt, you can move even fewer rocks."
- "I'm stopping you from practicing a future job you might have one day because it is bothering me."
- "I'm sending you to spend years learning a job that won't help the world as much as the job you have in mind."
- "I'm never trying things a different way that could help me,

even though you are always willing to try them with me. I'll even tease you for always being ready to try. Ha ha."

- "Stop playing imaginary games where you act like me to understand me better, so that you can help me someday! It's really annoying!"
- "If you don't do what I want, I will hurt your little sister."

Who would do it?

Bad Guys and Misguided People make the most use of Care Control Reasons. Misguided People like to put Learners in very bad situations to change them, so they like Care Control Reasons.

Pretending People and Workers use them too. They may wish to impress someone they think is a Self Guider. Maybe the person they thought was a Self Guider said something like, "Do whatever it takes to keep people from breaking that rule!" So the Worker or Pretending Person does so, but they are not smart enough to realize that perhaps keeping the rule from being broken was worse than sometimes letting people break it!

Wise Leaders and Self Guiders will probably not make use of any Care Control Reasons.

Here are some difficult choices you have if someone uses Care Control Reasons on you. No one knows the best way to handle it yet.

- **Think about why they would do it:** Are they doing it to please someone else who has control over their time, whom they still believe in, or for a reason they cannot remember? Is the thing you like actually dangerous or unhelpful and they just haven't told you why? Is there a chance it would cause you to die – since dying is much worse than discouraging you? Did they already tell you and you didn't believe them? Did they reach their thinking limit today and are unable to explain? Maybe it's not actually a Care Control Reason. Maybe their current goals are different than what you think they are, and accepting your help would actually hurt their goals. Example: If they are trying really hard to live a simple life to understand people who don't have much, then discouraging you from giving them expensive gifts would make sense.

This Learner really likes their teacher and tries to show it by making her a card. She takes the crayons to try to get the Learner to pay attention to the board. The Learner tries to make a deal with the teacher so her card could be finished.

- **Make them a deal:** "If you let me get better at helping you, I will let you hinder me for a while." It seems kind of strange you would have to make a deal with them, since they should already want you to help them, but that might be the only way to help them. Examples: "If I look at the board for five minutes, will you let me have my crayons to finish my picture for you?" "If I prepare a convincing presentation about why the job I want will make more money for our family than the job you want for me, will you rethink the decision you made for me?"

- **Try things their way:** For a while, you can try things their way. Hopefully, you can show them what effect their way has, and they will realize it. Unfortunately, since most people who use Care Control Reasons are not Wise Leaders, it will be no use. They won't keep track of their actions and will be unable to match them with their effects.

- **Give up being good:** Having things taken away from you when you're good can break your spirit and you may consider giving up being good altogether, to make the way you're being treated easier to deal with. You could begin to think, "If I stop caring about anyone, then I won't care if these things are taken away." This choice can, unfortunately, leave you less prepared to deal with people who actually treat you nicely in the future.

- **Hide what you like from them:** How much they can harm your ability to do good is based on how much they know about what you like. If they don't know what you like, then they can't take it away. Maybe you could even pretend to not be a good person around them.

- **Try to gain control of what they do with their time:** Since their caretakers didn't reason with them to get them to change, their caretakers must have tried to impel them. You could also try impelling them to get them to change. Saying things like, "Caretaker, I warned you in the past about hiding information that could help me help you. I'm afraid I'm going to have to limit the time I have to spend around you until you change," or "Caretaker, I'm very disappointed in you. You had a chance to explain what was on your mind when you took that toy away from your grandchild, but you did not. I'm afraid I'm going to have to limit the time you have around them." **Warning:** If you forget *why* you changed your goal to have control over what others do with their time (or you get changed into a different person), then you may accidentally become a **Pretending Person** or **Misguided Person**. These people keep on trying to have more and more control over other people's time, even if they don't deserve it. Make sure you only try to gain control over what people do with their time under the **right setting**.

- **Care about them less:** It will make it easier for you, when you hear about them harming themselves from their own actions, to care about them less. You could focus on caring about people who are easier to help and better at caring for themselves in the future.

    o You could be the kind of person who **views** those who use Care Control Reasons as **less than** everyone else, until they decide to change into the kind of person who doesn't use Care Control Reasons. If you are reaching your limits, perhaps it would be OK to only care about and value those who do not use Care Control Reasons *for now* (but don't forget why).

- **Let them hurt you,** but continue to want to help them someday, since it might still be possible that you are wrong about them, and it's not actually a Care Control Reason. You might only be able to help them in ways that give them more time in the day (like buying them gifts or making them food). If you do help them, they may wrongly interpret it as a success of their use of Care Control Reasons. Also, they may not appreciate your help as much as needier people would.

- **Talk to them about it:** Go up to them and tell them: "It feels like you are using a Care Control Reason on me, and I don't think that's right." Unfortunately, there is currently no way to talk about what everyone has on their mind when it comes to Care Control situations.

How a Learner Could Get Along With an Everything Knower

Getting along with an Everything Knowers is easy because they will let you know everything you need at every appropriate time.

They know exactly how you feel about something. If they tell you how you feel, then you know they are right.

They know what you like. If they tell you that you like something, you certainly do. If they tell you that you don't like something, well, then you certainly do not like it.

They know what you are. If they tell you what you are, you certainly are that. If they tell you you have a quality, you certainly do. If you put a lot of work into being someone else, it could be sad because all that time and energy was wasted.

There are no Everything Knowers in the world. If someone tells you how you feel, what you like, or who you are, you should not listen to them. No one currently has the ability to tell exactly what another person feels, likes, or indeed, what another person is.

Here are some other possible meanings when someone says you are something bad:

- They want to be alone, but they don't know how to say it.
- Someone they thought was a Self Guider said that.
- Someone who cares for them them said it to them, and they want to understand that person better by seeing how it feels to say it to others.

How a Learner Could Get Along With a Self Guider

Getting along with a Self Guider is also easy. You can try to communicate to them in lots of different ways, and they can understand. You can try to treat them how you want them to treat you, and they will understand and try to treat you the same. You can even think about them how you want them to think about *you*, and they can do that too!

Everything they do is something they like. If you do it too, you will impress them, and they will try to put as much energy into doing something you like.

You can demonstrate how much you believe in them and are committed to their cause, and they will have some good ideas on how to direct your energy to do the most good.

You can copy things they do that you don't understand yet, in order to communicate to them that you still believe they are Enoutable (they do everything for a good reason). That way, they will know you still believe in them.

If you have found a problem with a way they use, you can communicate it to them. If you make a good argument, they might be convinced to change their mind right away.

Sometimes you might think: "I'm uncertain about whether their way is for the best, and when I tried it, it certainly wasn't. Oh! Maybe their way didn't work because I didn't believe in it enough." If you completely forget your way and do things their way (believing in it 100%), it will either work and everything will be fine, or they will notice it failed despite all of your hard work, and offer to try things another way.

Unfortunately, no one like that exists. You should never believe in someone else's way 100%! In addition to not knowing the basics of how to do things other ways, they might not even be smart enough to realize that other ways exist. You may never meet someone to bring you back to your old ways. It may be better to remember things your way, even if it's really hard.

How a Learner Could Get Along With a Wise Leader

Wise Leaders like to talk to each other about what's working and what isn't with the people they lead. Sometimes they may try ways that cause you some harm. You may fear that the damage caused to your mind will never be known, and that the Wise Leader and the group will keep on using that harmful way on others. You may choose to keep the damage they caused your mind by walking around feeling awkward, sad, or hurt, or even telling them you are sad. They will want to have a nice talk and try to find out why. That way, maybe they will know what they did, realize it was a mistake, and say they are sorry. After they say sorry, you can focus on undoing the damage they have caused you.

If you do something bad on purpose, they take it to mean you are telling them something about yourself that would help you do more good than the bad thing you did. They are Pocobian. They are good at asking themselves, "What kind of messages would be so important that it would be worthwhile upsetting me or someone else for even a chance to communicate it?" and coming up with good answers. It's OK to use unconventional ways to communicate with them. If you are feeling like something is hindering you, and the only way you can think to communicate it at the time is to do something frustrating and hope they understand, then they will believe it's OK – however, they have limits to what they can understand, so you can only do this sometimes.

If you believe in them as much as you would a Self Guider or Everything Knower, they will feel partially responsible and guilty if they did not guide you the right way.

Unless there is a danger, you don't need to do anything until you are ready. They will not try to push you to use any of the ways of a Wise Leader until you want to. They will keep on leaving openings for you to jump in and join them if you want to, but they do not have strong feelings about whether you do or don't.

If they send you to do something that will take up a large part of your life, and its purpose is to help you, you can trust they put a lot of time considering what you would go through by doing it. If you then were to let them know it went badly, they would feel sad and use this as an opportunity to improve themselves.

Wise Leaders appreciate it if you admire them for particular qualities, but they don't like it when you think you could never have the qualities they have. They would want you to try to gain them, even if you think these qualities are beyond your reach.

How a Learner Could Get Along With Another Learner

If you see a Learner act like they believe something a lot, they are just trying it out. There are several possible reasons they would try it out:

- They are doing it because they want to better understand someone who cares for them, by acting like that person to see what kind of ideas they are thinking. If the Learner could better understand them, they might be able to help them some day.
- They might just be doing it because they want to **test** the way, and see if it really was for the best. A good way to see if someone is honest about being a Self Guider or a Wise Leader is to try out their way and see if it works.
- They may use this way because they trust a particular person with advantages over others.

Some have so much faith that a certain way works, they are willing to try it on other Learners. Play along with it and if it doesn't turn out to be for the best, they can usually figure it out. Sometimes, they might even talk like a Misguided Person. They will probably be able to figure it out by themselves. Hopefully.

Since there are no Everything Knowers or Self Guiders in the world, if they act very confident anyway, they are just seeing if being confident makes it work better. They don't actually know an Everything Knower or a Self Guider.

Teasing

Sometimes Learners might try teasing you by doing things like:

- Handing you something that could help you be your best, then when you reach for it, pulling it away.
- Trying to get your attention for something that you think could be important, but it isn't, and they are just making fun of you.

- Calling you dumb when you trust them as much as you would a **Self Guider** or **Wise Leader**.
- Telling you what you are, without knowing you well.

There are several kinds of **Learners** who do things like that:

1. A **Learner** who is smart enough to realize, all on their own, that treating people that way will not make the world a better place, but wants to know what to do or say to get people to stop by acting that way. They think you might know.
2. A **Learner** who doesn't know if it will make their environment a better, more thriving place.
3. A **Learner** who is trying to unconventionally communicate something with you, but doesn't know how to say it.
4. A **Learner** who learned from someone they trusted that treating people this way is the valid way to teach people the lesson of, "You shouldn't trust others to be a **Self Guider**." They may believe the person they trusted will be able to work out whether it's better or worse for the environment and change their mind.
5. A **Learner** who might actually be bad and wants to make the environment worse on purpose.

Since you probably don't know everything, you won't know what kind of **Learner** they are unless they leave enough clues for you to figure it out. Since it would not be a good idea to treat people like they are dumb or bad, you should treat them as though they are smart and good first. Maybe start with **Learner** 1, then **Learner** 2, 3, 4, and finally 5.

What to do for Learner 1 (the **Learner** who wants to know what you are supposed to say in this situation):

1. You can say what a **Self Guider** or an **Everything Knower** told you to say, if you know one.
2. Admit that you do not know what to say or do when someone does something like that, and that you don't know what they are thinking. Say that you are sorry and ask if they want to play something else.

What to do for Learner 2 (the **Learner** who doesn't know it's bad):

You can stop giving them chances for now, and give them a longer and longer time for them to realize their mistake.

Try doubling the time between chances you give them:

- try once
- try a second time
- try again when playing later
- try again tomorrow
- try again after two days
- try again after four days
- try again in a week
- try again in two weeks
- try again in a month
- try again in two months

Their Perspective When They Hand You Something and Pull It Back	Your Perspective When They Hand You Something and Pull It Back
"I wonder how long it will take them to stop reaching for the thing I'm handing them but pulling away."	"If they let me down here, I might have to view them as a **Pretending Person** from now on, and that will limit the amount of good we can do together. I hope they realize that they are risking their reputation with me next time they hand it to me. I will still reach for it..."

If they are not figuring it out, and you have already told them you don't know what to say, then you have some more options:

- Treat them how they treated you.
- Ask a caretaker for help.

If you treat them how they treat you, they might realize why it's bad, or they might not.

Asking a caretaker might help, but sometimes caretakers don't think the other **Learner** is doing anything wrong. Some might even get mad at both of you!

What to do for Learner 3 (a **Learner** who is trying to unconventionally communicate an idea with you):

If someone is teasing you to tell you something, there are usually two ideas that they would try to tell you:

1. That they view you as being in a lesser group than them.
2. Something else that they think could help you be a better person.

If the idea is that you belong to a lesser group than them, then you can either see things their way or not.

If they are a Wise Leader, then you could see it their way. However, since a Wise Leader would probably not tease someone to get that person to follow them, then you should probably reject that idea and go back to what you were doing.

If it's an idea of how you could change into a better person, then you have these two options:

1. Think like a Wise Leader. They would find a nice way to tell you if they knew how. Think about what that might be, and perhaps, let them help you become a better person.
2. Think that a person as good as you deserves to be told about it in a *nice* way, *not* by being teased. Choose not to accept their help.

A Learner's friend sees him with a runny nose. His friend makes fun of him by holding up a crayon to his nose and pretending it's boogers. Instead of getting mad as his friends for making fun of him, this Learner decides to think that his friends would say he should get a tissue in a nicer way if they were smart enough but, for now, he will accept their help as it is.

Since there are so few people in the world who know nice ways to say things to other people without teasing, perhaps it would be OK to accept their help.

Try to think about how you have treated them in the past. You might have done something to them that wasn't right. Maybe they are trying to communicate that it wasn't for the best. Try not to do stuff like that anymore, and maybe say you are sorry.

What to do for Learner 4 (less smart Learners who leave the thinking to someone else):

They are interested in making the world better, but they are not making the connections between a person's future actions and the way they have been treated. They leave the connecting to someone else whom they believe in – probably not a **Self Guider**. A **Self Guider** would have taught the **Learner** the best method. Whomever this person learned it from is likely unwilling to try things another way. You can also be sure that they will be upset with the problems that come from treating people this way without connecting them back to their action. You can also be sure that if someone treated this person with the same policy they have used to treat others, they would not enjoy it. The person they believe in may be a **Worker** or **Pretending Person**.

If they don't realize or pay attention to what effect it has on you, you could say something like:

- "I tried this game a lot and I don't like it."

- "When friends are playing together, I think they should do something they both like. I don't want to play it anymore, but if you want, I could tell you if I find someone who does."

- "My parents would be sad if they saw me playing this sort of game. Can we play a different game?"

What to do for Learner 5 (a **Learner** who's trying to make the world a worse place on purpose):

Still try not to see them as bad, but try not to be around them anymore. Think about how you could improve the way you handle it if someone else in the future were to treat you like they have. If you see them several years in the future, ask them if there was anything you could have done differently.

Ways of Deciding Who Gets What

Since we live in a place with limited resources, everybody can't have everything they want all the time. You may have to find a way to decide with other **Learners** who should have more food, a toy, or an experience first. Here are some ways to do it:

1. **Inside Way**: "It's good to give people what they need." Think about everything you have been through and everything they have been through, and decide what's best based on everything.

2. **Urgency Way**: "It's good to give people what they say they

need the most." Give it to the person who looks like they need it the most. Yelling, crying, looking sad, and stomping are some of the ways you could measure urgency.

3. **Equal Way**: "It's good to give people an equal amount of resources." Each person gets an equal about of whatever resource is available.

A mouse has way too much food for its size. An elephant does not have enough.

4. **Fair Way**: "It's good to give people fair amounts of resources." Each person gets as much of a resource as they need. (Example: Imagine you were trying to keep an elephant and a mouse from starving. If you gave them an equal amount of food, the elephant might starve, and the mouse would have more food than he needs. If you gave them a fair amount, no one would starve.)

5. **Burden Way**: "It's good to give people who are *very dedicated* to doing good what they need." Since the person who gets the resource will have an advantage over others, the person who would be willing to help the **most** with their advantage should get it. Each person lets it be known what they would do to make the world a better place if they got it. Example: "If you let me have this experience, I will use what I learn from it to help two kids to have this experience when I grow up."

The **Inside Way** would be the best way for people who have spent no time apart or who are Everything Knowers. But, if two people are apart and both have a very bad day, they would each think they should get what they want. So the Inside Way won't work sometimes. There would have to be other ways to decide who gets what. However, parts of this way may work if two people are very open and honest about their limits and resources.

The **Urgency Way** would be a good way to solve the problem of being apart. Whoever appears neediest should get whatever they need. There are some good and bad things about doing things this way too. If two people who use this way are very honest, it could work out well. There are several problems, however:

- If one comes under the care of a **Pretending Person** or **Misguided Person**, they will copy their sly and deceptive ways to make it seem like they need more than you.
- If the other person **views** you as **less than** others, they may think your frustrated feelings don't mean anything and aren't connected to making the world better.
- If one person thinks it will be best if they get the resource over another person, they will just be louder or cry more than the other person. If that other person thinks the same of themselves, they will both get louder and louder until everyone's ears hurt.

The **Equal Way** would be a good way to solve the problems of the Urgency Way. Everybody gets an equal share of the resource. If people are hungry, split the food. If they want an experience, they can take turns every five minutes to have that experience. The equal way might work well in a lot of cases. In others, it may not. If two kids want an orange, but one had never eaten an orange before in their life, while the other had just eaten one earlier that day, maybe it would be best to give the whole orange to the kid who had never had one before.

The **Fair Way** would be a good way to solve some of the problems of the Equal Way. Everybody gets a fair portion of what they need. Imagine if two people, one rich with $100, and one less rich with $10, want to build a road between their houses. They could both put in $10 to pay for it, but then the less rich one would have nothing left. If the less rich one paid $2 and the rich one paid $18, that would be a fair solution. But what if two kids want to share a stick in a fair or equal way, and the only reason one kid wants it is to hit others with it?

The **Burden Way** might be a good way to solve some problems with the other ways. The person who gets it is the one who's willing to help the most people with it. Unfortunately, a way to talk about it hasn't been invented yet. So you cannot look to any **Wise Leaders** for a way to have a conversation about it. There are still some questions on how a conversation like that would work.

- Would everybody have to say "…or something even better," whenever they make a deal? Since situations change, you might have the opportunity to do more good but in a

different way. Say you promised someone to feed 10 hungry people in the future if a person gave you their last candy bar. However, in the future, you live in a world where everyone is well fed, so instead, you build a playground for kids.
    - o Does that count as a fair trade?
    - o Should they have said, "…or something even better"?
    - o Should everyone agree that they don't need to say "…or something even better" when they use the Burden Way?
- Could you trade burdens with other people?
- If you are unlucky and never get the resources to repay your burden, but your friends get lucky, is it OK if they repay your burden for you?

Balance

People have poor balance when they start learning to walk. They may overshoot their steps and fall backwards. Then they'll say, "I'm not gonna do that again," and next time they undershoot their steps and fall forward. The time after that, they overdo it again and fall backward again. **Learners** may also have trouble trying to balance when-to-take and when-to-give, when they are trying to decide who gets what. Sometimes, they might overshoot and take too much. Sometimes, they might undershoot and take too little. Just because they make a mistake, it doesn't mean they are selfish.

Bothering

If someone is doing something that bothers you, you could ask them to stop. If they keep on doing it, it might be an unconventional way of saying, "I don't think you should be so bothered by it." Then you could:

1. Try putting the energy you have used being bothered by it, into not being bothered anymore and see what happens.
2. Tell them the bad thing that happened last time someone did the thing that bothered you. (Example: "The last time someone threw sand at me, some got into my ear.")
3. Let them know that you are a limited person and have trouble changing how you feel when someone does something like that. Tell them that you will try not to be bothered by it sometime in the future, but it would really help if they stopped for now.
4. Get into a conflict (see below.)

Threats and Conflict

Sometimes **Learners** say things like, "If you don't stop doing that and leave me alone, I will hurt you."

You might be thinking, "People shouldn't threaten to hurt others. I should carry on anyway as an unconventional way to communicate that they shouldn't hurt others!"

Maybe they like to hurt people and are just looking for a chance to hurt someone. Doing something like that might be one way to get them to stop – or might they be thinking something else?

They may be thinking, "I really think that being left alone right now would be for the best," and "I don't actually want to hurt anyone, but if I say I do, they will leave me alone for sure!"

Maybe they are asking for something that everyone might deserve. (Do **Learners** deserve some time alone sometimes? Since we live in a world where people have **limits**, then the answer is probably yes.) In that case, you could say, "Thanks for letting me know you want to be left alone." Then leave them alone without minding how harshly they communicated it. They will figure out by themselves that they don't need to threaten you next time, since they are probably good and smart.

Things that every **Learner** may deserve that might be for the best:

Being left alone:	"Nope, I'm gonna keep following you."	"Thanks for letting me know you want to be left alone."
Being called their own name:	"Nope, I'm going to keep calling you shorty."	"Thanks for letting me know you want to be called James."
Having a chance to be treated how they want:	"You want to be Super-hero team leader? No, I'm always the leader."	"Alright, you can have a turn being the leader."
Having you stop doing something bothersome that can easily be stopped:	"You want me to stop playing with that noisy toy? Why don't you try being not so bothered by the noise first?"	"Alright, I'll stop playing this and do something else. Thanks for letting me know."

Maybe you can add or remove different things from this list if the other **Learner** agrees to it. Example: You could try to decide that everyone should keep on doing something, even if it bothers someone else, and see how that works. The next time someone does something that bothers someone else, they should just try to ignore it. Some friends just call each other odd nicknames all the time and aren't bothered by it (but a **Self Guider** would probably be happy if they saw you giving everyone a chance to be treated how they wished).

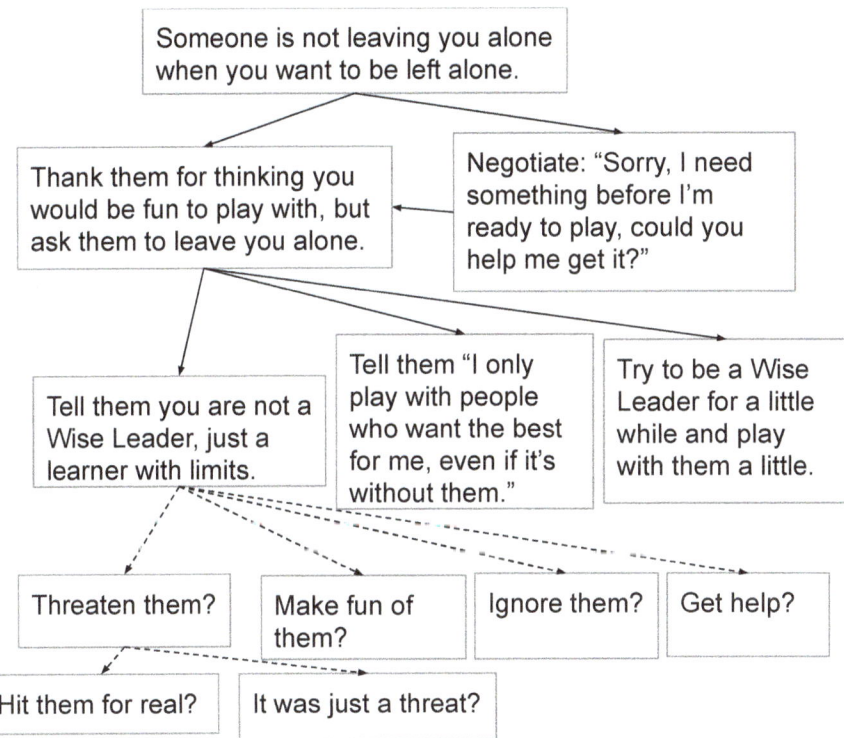

There are lots of things you could try to get someone to leave you alone.

First, you could try one of these choices:

1. You could say, "Thank you for thinking I would be fun to play with, but I would rather play by myself now." This lets them know you still think they are a good person now, and have a chance to be really great in the future.

2. Negotiate: Ask yourself, "I don't want to play with them now, but what would need to change before I feel like it? Can they help me get it?" If you think of something, then

you could tell them: "Sorry, but I need _____ before I'm ready to play. Could you help me get it?" Example: "Sorry, I need to finish planting my flowers before I'm ready to play. Can you help me?" You can use some ideas from the different **ways to decide who gets what**: the Equal Way, the Fair Way, and the Burden Way. Examples of each: **The Equal Way**: "I will play with you for five minutes if you leave me alone for five minutes," or "I will play the game you want for five minutes if you play a game I want for five minutes." **The Fair Way**: "I am really tired because I had to spend time with a Misguided Person today. I can play with you if we play what I want." **The Burden Way**: "I'll play with you, but you have to *promise* that the next three times someone wants to play with you, when you would rather be alone, you *still* play with them, OK?"

If they still won't leave you alone, you can try three more choices:

1. Tell them, "I'm not a Wise Leader. I am just a Learner with limits, so I don't know enough to help you yet – sorry. If you let me have some time alone to think, maybe I can think of a way to help someone like you, but it might take a while." This gives them some information from this book about how some people have negative qualities, and lets them know that you are a person with some negative qualities. They might really need that information in order for them to be their best.

2. "Sorry, I only spend time with people who want the best for me, even if it's without them." This lets them know that you only spend time with people who want you to become your best self. If they want to spend time with you in the future, then they will have to change into that kind of person.

3. Give their perspective a try. Maybe you actually do have enough energy to play with them? Say something like, "Wow, it really looks like you *need* someone to play with you right now," to let them know you are putting a lot of thought into what they are going through, then try to be a Wise Leader and play with them as a Wise Leader would. Maybe you might even learn something new from playing with them.

If they still keep bothering you after you want to be left alone, what to do next is very uncertain. Without an Everything Knower or Self Guider's help, no one really knows the best way to handle it.

1. Would it be best to threaten them next? What would be best for the world? If someone didn't threaten them, would they keep on going to people and discouraging them from being their best? If you make a threat by saying, "If you don't leave me alone, I'll hit you," does that mean you have to hit them afterward? If people follow the way of, "Lying is bad," then should you? What if a **Pretending Person** who used the way, "If someone hits someone else, that proves they are bad!" saw you hitting them and did not want to understand the full situation? They would treat you like you were bad.
2. Should you make fun of them? Say something you don't mean, like, "Oh yea, I really want to play with someone who keeps bothering me. Ha ha, yeah *right!*"? Should you even call them names? Would it be less harmful than hitting them? Would it be for the best? No one knows yet.
3. Would ignoring them be for the best?
4. Should you get help? Are there any good people around whose job it is to help? Are there any caretakers? Yelling really loud for help might also be a good idea. Should getting help always be your first choice if you can?

How a Learner Could Get Along With a Worker

To think about how to treat a **Worker**, you have to imagine how you would feel if you decided to stop improving. What would you have to go through in order to be convinced to stop improving? Many **Workers** have probably gone through something like that. They may have wanted to stay a **Learner**, but were forced to become a **Worker** too soon. They might have even wanted to be a **Wise Leader**, but realized they were not smart enough to become one, or some other reason stopped them, and they had to make this choice.

Can You Convince Them It's OK to Be a Learner Again?

For some it is possible. For some, there is nothing you can do to convince them it's OK to be a **Learner**.

Talking to Them

Don't call someone a **Worker** if you find out they are one. They do not like that kind of conversation.

If they ask you a general question, ask it back to them after you answer.

Be careful, sometimes it doesn't work.

If they wish you a good time, wish it back to them too.

Be careful, sometimes it doesn't apply.

If you break one of their rules of how they get along with others, it will upset them if you say it out loud. Saying things like this would make them upset:

- "Oops, I forgot, I was supposed to ask your name after you asked mine."
- "Oops, I forgot, I wasn't supposed to say, 'I am very sad,' after you asked me, 'How are you today?' I was supposed to say, 'I am good,' even though it was not true."

They may think you are making fun of them for not being able to be a Self Guider and it hurts their feelings, or maybe they know someone who they really trusted who gets upset at things like that. If you make one of these mistakes, don't worry about it. You should focus on being better to help the world one day. If you want to be a Wise Leader someday, it might be a good idea to practice making Workers happy, though.

You might think that all Workers like their job, but some Workers may not like talking about their job. They may not even like to talk about new ways to get their job done. They may have had to make some hard decisions, and decided to take a job they didn't even like. You should talk about other things (like their environment spaces) if you don't want to upset them too much.

Wise Leaders don't expect you to do things that you aren't ready to do. They predict the negative effects it could have on you. With some Workers, they will want you to jump into their ways as soon as you are able, even if it hinders your abilities. If you don't and it upsets them, it's OK. It's better for a Worker to be upset than a Learner to be discouraged from achieving their potential.

A Worker Who Cares for You

If a Worker is caring for you, and it's their job, how do you tell them their ways aren't working and let them know other ways might be worth trying? You would have to consider their **Boss.** Their boss has control over what the Worker does with their time, and can make up punishments so Workers are **impelled** by the boss to keep doing what the boss wants.

If their boss is a Self Guider, there are lots of things that would convince them to change their ways:

- If they see that a way is not making the environment thrive.
- They test to see how one way makes a thriving environment compared to another way, and choose the best one.
- Lots of people try unconventional ways of communicating how a way hinders their ability to do good and be their best

(sometimes called a rebellion or starting a revolution).

- They can see their **Workers** are discouraged in a meeting and talk about how to make them not so discouraged.

If their boss is a **Pretending Person** or a **Worker**, then there are only certain things that will convince them to change their way:

- If they get ordered to give it a try or else they will get fired.
- If a lot of people who give them money are complaining.

Sometimes a **Worker** will "try" to stop you from doing something you both know is healthy and helps you to become a better person, like helping the **Worker** sweep the floor, or training for an emergency situation by jumping off a tall thing. They don't actually stop you, however, and instead let you do it. Their boss has made a **Rule** that they should stop people like you from doing that action, even though anyone who knows you *knows* that you are able to handle it. You have to watch them closely to see if they are telling you not to do something because it's their job. If you tell other people the **Worker** let you do that healthy activity when they should have stopped you, the **Worker** may get in trouble with their boss. They will probably not realize that you are trying to help them understand that, since nothing went wrong, it might be good to let you and others do it in the future.

A Worker acts like they are trying to stop a Learner from coming into a fun land. A rule says they are too young to come in, so it seems like they are following the rules. The Worker looks away and winks at the Learner as if to say the Learner could come in if they want to because following the rules this time won't make for a better world.

Whoever made the rule might not be an Everything Knower, Self Guider, Wise Leader, or even a Learner. They might be a Worker or even someone who is Pretending! If anything bad were to happen from you doing the act anyway, the **Boss or Rule Maker** would hear about it. They would be mad at the Worker who was caring for you. If more bad things happened, the Worker could lose their job and not have money to afford food or a home. If something good happened when you did the act that helped you achieve your potential and do good in the future, the Rule Maker would not hear about it and may not even care, since lots of Bosses are Workers or Pretending People.

Disappointingly, the Worker would not be rewarded, nor would they have helped to influence the future decisions of the Rule Maker if something really good had actually come about from your action. Bosses are usually Workers or Pretending People so they won't be interested anyway.

Workers Who Don't Care for You

Sometimes, Workers don't want to play or talk to young Learners at all. It's because there are still Bad Guys in the world. Sometimes people who aren't Bad Guys get accused of being Bad Guys and go to jail too. Bad Guys like to get close to young Learners to hurt them. If they are caught, then they have to go to jail. Some Workers think, "If I just avoid young Learners entirely, then I won't get accused and go to jail." That is why some Workers don't want to play or talk to you; not because something is wrong with you, but because there are Bad Guys and because the most common practice for catching Bad Guys also catches a few innocent Workers.

Trying Things Your Way

Sometimes, Workers try to help you by sending you to do something that will take time away from your current goals. When they set you to a task, you have to remember that they aren't likely to have thought it out very well, especially from your perspective. Don't expect them to be inclined to try things your way in return. Their own actions are likely just a repetition of something they saw done by a person they admire. If you let them know it went badly, they might say they heard it worked for someone else.

Some Workers might be willing to try things another way under very particular circumstances. Say they had a business deal with people of a different culture who lived far away, and they had to visit there occasionally. They would be willing to try hard to understand this culture's way in this situation. That doesn't mean they love people in different countries who own businesses more than they love you. They love you in a different way. Since they do not lead an accountable life, like a **Self Guider**, they are not able to explain exactly what that means.

If you really wanted your caretakers to try things your way, then you could try to have control of your own business and culture. Then invite them to come to you. An easier way would be to find people who are more open to trying things differently. One thing that might work for some **Workers** is making a deal with them. Tell them something like: "If you rethink your way, I'll do what you want," or "I had a turn doing things your way, and now it's your turn to do things my way."

Exercises: Say you give these two test questions to each of the types of people you might meet, and they have to answer honestly. On a separate piece of paper, write down what each one would answer.

Question 1. How long would I have to be not naughty until you think of a better way to handle it the next time I am naughty?

- A. None, I will do the right thing the first time.
- B. Between a moment to an hour.
- C. Between a few hours to a week.
- D. Between a week to a month.
- E. Several years or less if someone explains it to me.
- F. I deserve to care for people who are never naughty, even if it hinders their potential.

Everything Knower _____

Self Guider _____

Wise Leader _____

Learner _____

Worker _____

Pretending Person _____

Answers:

Everything Knower A
Self Guider B
Wise Leader C
Learner D
Worker E
Pretending Person F

Question 2: Someone you care for has an idea for a potentially better way to live. How well said and far along would the idea have to be before you are willing to honestly consider it?

- A. They just have to think it.
- B. They can try to tell me without really knowing how, and I will help them work out how to say it.
- C. I will try my best to understand, but I may make mistakes.
- D. Written down with no errors, or presented in a very entertaining way.
- E. We agree to play about it or test it on a town-sized group of people and ensure that it still works.
- F. If I have to try it to do my job, or I see lots of my friends doing it.
- G. No amount of effort will ever be good enough for me.

Everything Knower _____

Self Guider _____

Wise Leader _____

Learner _____

Worker _____

Pretending Person _____

Answers:

A	Everything Knower
B	Self Guider
C	Wise Leader
D	Learner
F	Worker
G	Pretending Person

Answer Explanation: Answer D isn't used. If you make a song, play, poem, movie, or words without any mistakes, most caretakers would say "Good job," or "You could do this for a living!" without thinking about trying things another way. It may work on busy **Wise Leaders** or **Self Guiders** who don't care for you, if you want to stand out to get their attention.

Trying to Make Workers Happy

Sometimes, Workers are not smart enough to know what's going on inside you and how that will affect how pleased they are with you in the future. If you plan on doing something that you hope will make them very proud of you someday, you might have to do some things to make them a bit mad or sad now. Even if you reach your goals, they may never realize those times they were mad or sad were traded for making them really happy later.

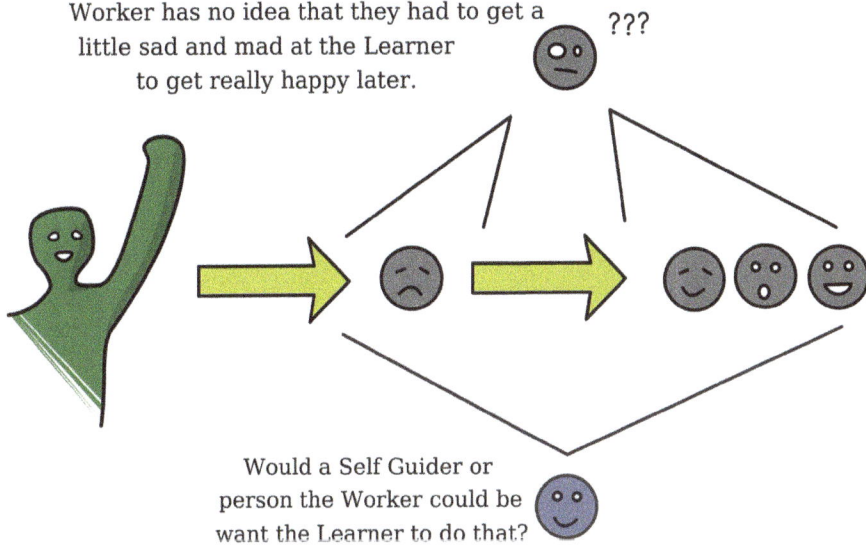

If your caretakers don't seem to realize you are making them sad/mad for a very good reason, you have two options:

1. Keep on making them a little sad so they can be very happy later.
2. Only make them a little happy later.

If they show any progress in self-improvement, once they get closer to being a Self Guider, then they might understand why you had to do those things, and you may want to choose option 1 more. If they show very little progress, maybe choose option 2 more.

You might get very frustrated trying to figure out why a Worker doesn't tell you what they know, in order to help you. It might save them from being mad at you. Just remember, they might not know why they do the things they do, and even if they did, they would not know how to put it into words to tell you.

How a Learner Can Get Along With a Pretending Person

Pretending People's way of thinking usually starts with, "I want something from this other person that will help me, but maybe won't make the world a better place. I should make it *seem* like it will make the world a better place." They try to alter their views, ways, values, and perspective of the world to try to get what they are really after. You should focus on finding the **origin idea** behind their actions.

With a **Pretending Person**, whenever they tell you something or do something, you always have to ask yourself:

1. How can they see it?
2. How can they know it?
3. Are they smart enough to figure it out by themselves?
4. Do they even care how much good I can do in the future?

If they tell you they can see or hear something beyond what a normal person's eyes can see or ears can hear, they might be trying to trick you.

If they act like they have knowledge beyond a normal person's ability to know, they might also be trying to trick you. If they say they have knowledge about *you*, without getting to know you very well, then you know they might be trying to trick you.

If they say they have figured something out that is outside of their normal ability, and act confidently that it is true, they might be trying to trick you.

If they do something that makes it seem like they care about you being your best self or are really sorry for how they treated you in the past, then they might have changed from being a **Pretending Person** or… they might be trying to trick you again!

It can be really bothersome thinking about these things every time they say or do something. You might feel like you are not doing your best if you have to use so much energy to think about these things. You are doing the most good, though, because thinking these things will probably help you do more good.

Exercise 1: On another piece of paper, mark the **real reason** a **Pretending Person** would treat you in the way listed below:

1. A man comes up to you and says: "Hey kid, I got a toy here I really think you would like. Why don't you try it?"

    A. He heard about you from someone else you know well, and then he sat down and thought really hard about which toys would help you be your best, and believes he has one that might.

    B. His boss pays him based on how many of this particular toy he sells to kids. He acts like he knows you to trick you. He doesn't actually care if it helps you to be your best. He doesn't even care that his tricks could lead people to distrust each other more, or to even distrust **Wise Leaders** who actually want to help people.

2. Someone your age sees you sitting alone. They ask about what you like to do for fun, and they say, "Wow, me too," for everything that you tell them. They invite you over to the park to do those things.

    A. They just want you to come to the park to make fun of you with their friends, so you seem less than them. They thought, "What would I have to say or do to get that **Learner** to come to the park the quickest?" and then they did that. They don't actually like to do the things you described.

    B. By luck, they are interested in all the same things that you are, and follow the way of, "It's good to be around people with the same interests, so you can push them further," and that's why they invited you to the park.

3. Someone says, "I know you work *so hard*. Don't you think you deserve a rest?" Then they tell you about a group they belong to and want you to join and help out.

    A. They somehow know how hard you've been working your whole life to be a good person. The group they want you to join has people that could make the world a better place.

B. Someone said that to them, so they joined the group. Now they say it to other people. They don't actually know how hard you've been working. The group's leader said they need more members to *believe* in them before something good happens, but that day may never come.

Answers:

1:B; 2:A; 3:B

Exercise 2: On another piece of paper, mark the **origin idea** behind the following actions a **Pretending Person** would have.

1. A group of people are very good at building things with rocks. One day, someone discovers metal. One leader, the son of the best rock worker, thinks using metal is a very bad idea.

    A. "I have to make sure we live in the best environment that helps our group succeed, and using rock is the best."

    B. "I have to make sure this is a perfect environment where my caretaker will be most comfortable and familiar. I have to make sure he is still useful."

2. You hear someone say, "I'm not gonna try things your way. I believe every way is wrong except my own."

    A. "It was hard enough learning the ins and outs of the ways I have now. I am not smart enough to imagine the ins and outs of the world you are showing me, so I will stay in the world I'm familiar with. If I just believe my ways are right, it will be easier for me."

    B. "I have the knowledge of a **Self Guider**, and I know the ways I use are the best ways for everyone and would make for the best world."

3. Someone is passionately fighting in a war and has already destroyed three enemies. He doesn't try to watch the news and just does what he's told.

    A. "I don't need to read the news or do lots of research because I know everything, and I know I am on the right side, and winning will be for the best!"

    B. "I can't read the news, and I have to avoid it. If I find out I have been tricked and I actually killed three good people... I don't even know what I would do. I don't want to think about it."

Answers: 1:B; 2:A; 3:B

Whenever someone says something, normally you might think, "Hmm, they are either lying or telling the truth." There is a third option: not knowing or **Reserving Judgment** until you know more. Some people's way is, "Be surprised or hurt if someone doesn't believe you." If someone is surprised and hurt when you don't believe them, you can now tell them that you think they are an honest person, but you are just **reserving judgment** until you know more.

Pretending People and Rules

Pretending People like to lie about why a rule is there, or make up a reason on the spot. Even if you change your job to prove that they are wrong, they may just make up a different reason. The real reason is that they are not a **Self Guider** and are uncomfortable thinking about how the world would work if that rule was gone. They have never heard of anyone that was in charge of them changing their mind. They don't know if it's OK to defy their caretaker's way. They will not bring your proof to their boss or rule maker, and will not suggest a new way.

Exercise: Say you ask a caretaker why there is a rule. What they tell you doesn't sound quite right. You decide to go about proving them wrong. On another piece of paper, match what happens to the type of person you would meet.

1. **Self Guider**	A.	They will bring up your proof with their friends and will try to have the rule changed.
2. **Wise Leader**	B.	They made up a reason for the rule. If you prove they are wrong, they will make up another reason or get frustrated and do something unexpected.
3. Worker	C.	They will say, "That's just the way things are," when you ask them why. You won't even get a chance to prove them wrong.
4. **Pretending Person**	D.	When you ask them, they get really mad at you. They will call you bad for "questioning me" and "questioning authority." You are not bad, though, because you are just trying to help.
5. **Misguided Person**	E.	All you have to do is prove them wrong, then they will try things a different way.

Answers:
1:E; 2:A; 3:C; 4:B; 5:D

How Often to Give Pretending People Another Chance

Sometimes you might see a **Pretending Person** do something that is very surprising. They might **impel** you to do or not do something, make up a **Care Control Reason**, or something even more unexpected than those. The result is that it harms your relationship and trust in them, and harms your potential to do good and maybe even their own potential to do good.

When you make a mistake like that, you usually realize it after thinking about it. You would want your dear ones to give you another chance to try it again. Since you don't want to treat the **Pretending Person** like they are not smart enough to figure it out, you keep on giving them more chances. Surely they will figure it out if they take some time to think about it? But, when you keep on doing it, it seems they do not rethink it! You get really tired and drained from giving them another chance all the time. How often should you give them another chance?

Try doubling the gap between the times you gave them another chance:

- try once
- try again tomorrow

- try again after two days
- try again after four days
- try again in a week
- try again in two weeks
- try again in a month
- try again in two months
- try again in four months
- try again in eight months
- try again in a year
- try again in two years
- try again in four years

Hopefully, someone realizes something and changes their ways, or hopefully, you will know the words to talk about it someday, instead of giving them more chances.

Communicating With Pretending People Based on the Damage They Cause You

You can keep the damage they cause your mind, like how you would with a Wise Leader. You can walk around feeling awkward, sad, or hurt. Maybe if someone else notices, they can talk to the Pretending Person about their ways and what to change. That way, if you keep on being hurt, you will eventually help others not to be hurt in the future. It seems like a very good and selfless thought to give up your future to help the future of others.

- In this world, scientists and other people in charge are just starting to collect information on how treating other people affects them (like measuring how treating or caring for kids a certain way affects the success of a whole school or a whole country!). But, currently, most people ask "What's wrong with them?" instead of asking "What happened or keeps happening to them to make them act like that?". If you think that there isn't any information being collected about how you are treated and what effect it has, maybe you should not keep the damage.

- Also, in this world, it is very common to encounter people who are Pretending to be leaders. If you keep the damage they cause you as a way of asking for help, it's unlikely that anyone will understand what ways the Pretending Person used on you. People who Pretend also do not like it when others question their ways. If it's not against the law, they will probably keep doing it anyway. Even if it is against the law in one place, some Pretending People might move to another place rather than rethink their way!

- It's nice that a **Pretending Person** can experience the unpleasant results of their own actions. Unfortunately, they are **just not smart enough** to connect your behavior with something they did to you in the past.
- If someone very young sees you with the damage they gave you – and they think you are a **Self Guider** – they will believe it's OK to think and act like that.

Considering these ideas, it might be more selfless and good to try to recover from the damage **Pretending People** give you, instead of keeping it. Although it might be *very upsetting* to hear that a **Pretending Person** feels like they are responsible for your success if you do succeed, you might have to think of something to say to them if they do.

Communicating Concepts in Other Ways

You might think most people would rethink things that make them feel overwhelmed, but **Pretending People** are not really the ones to do that.

Thoughts a **Wise Leader** Might Have	Thoughts a **Pretending Person** Might Have
"It's really tiring being upset when they make that noise all the time. Hmm… Oh! Maybe instead of using so much energy to be upset, I could use that energy to become the kind of person who isn't bothered when people make that noise!"	"That noise is making me madder and madder. They do not listen when I tell them to stop. I will have to take away more and more things they like to get them to stop!"
"Being angry when they do that doesn't seem to be working, Hmm… Oh! Maybe I should try to be proud of them when they do that and see how that goes!"	"Why do they do that?! What's wrong with them?"

"When I didn't tell them the weak areas of the human body, so they could avoid them, they hit people there anyway. Hmm... Oh! maybe if I had told them earlier, they would have tried to avoid those areas! Whoops, I guess it's kind of my fault..."

"They hit a person's weak areas when I didn't tell them, so they proved they are horrible and they did not deserve to have this information anyway!"

Can a Pretending Person Be Convinced to Try Other Ways?

The thoughts of a Wise Leader are not the typical thoughts of a Pretending Person. They might be beyond your ability to convince because:

- **Pretending People** don't like to admit they are not able to change their mind about something.
- They don't know they have the power to not care about something or change how they feel about something.
- They follow the way of "People I care for cannot be the source of any useful ideas."
- They might secretly be against the ideas of people below a certain age.
- Their way is to only listen to those who have more control over how other people spend their time.
- Their way is to only listen to those who have something they want.
- Their way is to not consider ideas unless they are said with an adult voice.
- Their way is to only communicate with words.
- They are thinking, "Since no one bothered to try my ways when I was young, why should I bother to try other people's ways now?"
- All of their friends feel that way about it. If they change ways, their friends might not like them anymore, and they will feel lonely.
- Someone they trusted when they were very young felt a particular way, and they are worried bad things will happen if they defy those ways!

- Someone told them when they were young that people are stupid if they don't know that a certain way is the correct way. They trusted them and didn't want to be seen as stupid, so they kept that way.
- They follow the way of "It's good to judge parents on everything their kids do." They are worried that people will judge them poorly, based on what you do.
- They are worried that they will have fewer opportunities to help you grow if the people who give opportunities judge them poorly.
- If they let you do annoying things around them, they think you will grow used to doing that, and upset many **Learners** and hinder their ability to do good. They don't think you are smart enough to know to treat different people differently.

You might think someone who cares for you could easily change how they feel when certain things happen, but it is very *very* hard for them. It might even be impossible! They have **Waylock**.

Instead of re-evaluating the effect of their actions on you, or considering the reasons behind your action, they may give you a **negative label**. Some common negative labels are "mean," "noisy," "disrespectful," "shy," "liar," or "bad." You are not any of those things, though.

Since they don't play with you so you can learn all the ways you could respond to an action, everything you can think of doing will cause them to give you a negative label (even doing nothing may result in them giving you a negative label!). You might have to choose the negative label that you think will hinder you the least.

It might be sad if an **Everything Knower**, a **Self Guider**, or a **Wise Leader** gave you a negative label. But it's very normal for **Pretending People** to give negative labels before they understand what's going on, so it's not worth getting distressed over. Also, they:

- **Sometimes forget:** They won't remember that they gave you a negative label a few years or even months or days from now.
- **Don't do much good in their spare time:** They do nothing worthwhile that you would want to be invited to join. Even if they don't like you, it doesn't matter, because there aren't any good works they do that you could help them with.
- **Never earn a Wise Leader's trust:** Even if a **Wise Leader** heard a **Pretending Person** say a **Learner** had a negative

quality, the Wise Leader would probably say something like, "I'll reserve judgment until I meet them myself."

Considering these ideas, it might be a good idea not to be sad when a Pretending Person gives you a negative label.

When Caretakers Take Away Things You Really Need

If you and your friends are Learners on the path to becoming Wise Leaders to do lots of good someday, you may need lots of resources and experiences to play around with, to get a whole understanding of the world. Sometimes when you go for a particular experience, a Pretending Person says you can't because it is bad, and you are bad for trying to experience it. They also may try to create punishments so that you are **impelled** from doing it. They don't tell you why it's bad, and it's also very easy to see that they are mistaken. Even if it was bad for one of the Learners, it could still help the others be the best Wise Leader they could be someday. Things like:

- Talking to your friends about something more important than what a Pretending Person wants you to talk about.
- Playing with your friends.
- Solving problems in new ways.
- Playing with an old tire.
- Playing in the mud.
- Reading about how the world works.
- Listening in on how caretakers secretly talk to each other about problems you've created.
- Wiggling around.

You have some options on ways to approach what they are doing to you:

1. **Mourning Approach**: Enduring the loss of this resource or experience and still trying to continue along the path of a Wise Leader who will one day do good.
2. **Sneaky Approach**: Trying to keep on having the experience by sneaking around, but still intending to be a Wise Leader to do good.
3. **Enforce Approach**: Trying to stop other people using this resource or experience to impress the Pretending Person

enough that they will:

A. Come to you for advice and you can finally tell them, "Hmm, I think this way wasn't for the best and was actually really discouraging."

B. Help them see how the end result of their actions did not make for a thriving environment.

C. Make you the new leader so you can get rid of their way.

4. **Deviant Approach** (sometimes called rebelling): Sacrificing your potential to be a **Wise Leader** and do the most good in exchange for helping future **Learners** who wish to be **Wise Leaders**. Change yourself into someone who enjoys this experience. Force the **Pretending Person** to get overwhelmed with trying to stop people from having this experience and have the **Pretending Person** finally realize it was a bad idea to ban it.

The Pretending People banned wiggling around and being silly for some reason they won't share. So many Learners have broken the rule and filled the jail for wiggle kids that the Pretending People will hopefully consider rethinking having this rule in the first place.

Ins and Outs of the Mourning Approach

You might be sad that you were not able to try your best to do good. At least you can shake off whatever negative label they give you. If you see people in the future who took this option, you might notice they still want to experience it but have forgotten why they wanted to. If they try it now, it would not benefit them as much as when they were younger.

Ins and Outs of the Sneaky Approach

Now you have to put some energy into being deceptive. After you are done with this approach, you can move on. If you see people in the future who have taken this option, you might have noticed that instead of trying to deceive just **Pretending People** and only under the **right setting**, they are deceptive to everyone! They are becoming a **Pretending Person** themselves! If you take this option, remember that you only need to deceive those who prove themselves to be a **Pretending Person**.

Another mistake people make is that they do *not* move *on* to other things when they are done with it, and they accidentally move to the deviant approach instead of sticking with the sneaky approach. If you decide to take this option, remember to **get bored** with the experience and **move on** to other things!

Ins and Outs of the Enforce Approach

You should probably not take this approach. **Pretending People's** ways are usually not worth spreading. If you do, now you have to be an enforcer of their way. You will have to do things that will knowingly harm people's potential so that you can impress the **Pretending Person**. Things like:

- Saying, "Oh that makes sense," when the **Pretending Person** tells you their way (even before you understand it and compare it to many other ways).

- Saying, "Everyone who doesn't see this is the right way is dumb – ha ha," when the **Pretending Person** tells you their way.

- Saying, "If you don't understand this way is the best, well, it's probably too complicated for you," when someone asks you why you act like the **Pretending Person** (even though the **Pretending Person** didn't put as much thought into it as a **Self Guider**).

- Saying something like, "Obviously, even a baby could see this is the right way," when someone asks you why you act like the **Pretending Person** (even though smart and good people might come up with different ways that might also be good ideas).

- Making things difficult by forcefully impelling others from using other ways.

- Telling on the **Learners** who performed the banned action, so the **Pretending Person** can try to forcefully impel them to discourage them.

- **Viewing** people who use other ways as **less than** people who do things the Pretending Person's way.

- Using unconventional ways to communicate or teasing, when people try the banned way.

These might work if the Pretending Person is like a Scientist. A Scientist would accept the results of an experiment on people to see if it harmed them, but they would need to make sure everyone was trying it that way so they got accurate results. Pretending People do not keep track of their ways to see if they harm people.

These also might work if the Pretending Person matched everyone's effort and faith in the enforcing of their ways into imagining how their subjects feel when useful experiences are kept from them. Then they would realize their ways are discouraging. Unfortunately, Pretending People are not able to think like that anymore.

If they truly are a Pretending Person, then you know they **need help** before your attempts to make an impression on them have any effect. Before they get the help they need, they will not ask you for advice, imagine how their subjects feel, or keep track of the effects of their ways.

Even if the Pretending Person did ask your advice, many people who follow this path forget what they wanted to say or how to say it (how to talk about **ways** mostly hasn't been invented yet). So, if you tell the Pretending Person, "I don't think this way is for the best," and they ask, "Which way?" you will be unable to communicate which way you mean.

Many people who take the Enforce Approach think the Pretending Person is testing their commitment to their way, so they continue to support the Pretending Person's way.

Even if you are dedicated enough for the Pretending Person to choose you as the new leader, many new leaders forget what they were going to do, because they have put so much energy into the Pretending Person's way. It may have been many many years ago, and now they have completely forgotten their own way.

Ins and Outs of the Deviant Approach

Giving up your potential to do good so others can is a great sacrifice. Perhaps, if enough people use the Deviant Approach, the Pretending Person will be overwhelmed with trying to create difficulties to forcefully impel you to stop, so they have to give up. Unfortunately, people who look up to you and think you're a **Self Guider** will wonder why you are the kind of person who really really likes this way. It might be difficult to say, "I'm not a **Self Guider**. I'm just doing it to help a **Pretending Person** realize their mistake in thinking it's bad."

Pretending People do not typically think in terms of:

- "Wow! They would give up all their potential just to try to communicate something important to me, maybe… maybe I should listen."
- "Oh no, if I hadn't called them bad for doing that all those years ago, they might have become a **Wise Leader** and have done lots of good – whoops."

They usually think in terms of:

- "Look at what they have become from doing that thing. Oh no, I should have tried harder to stop them from doing it in the first place!"
- "Hmm, they must be dumb to see it as not good. I will have to force them not to do it."

Also, many people who take this option forget they took it to help **Learners** reach their potential to be a **Wise Leader**. They also sometimes end up choosing ways that hurt **Learners**. They overdo it with liking the experience so much and teasing **Pretending People** with it so much, that they end up teasing everyone, even **Learners**!

Exercises: Write down your answers to these questions on another piece of paper.

1. Say a **Pretending Person** doesn't like it when a **Learner** tells on other **Learners** when they break one of their rules. Which way to handle it would they probably NEVER think of on their own, no matter how much you believe in them?

    A. They give the **Learner** telling on other **Learners** the **negative label** of "tattle tail," and get mad at them and try to make them feel bad.

    B. They admit to the **Learner** that they are a **Pretending Person**, and tell them that means it's OK to **not** spread their ways to others. They would say they are sorry for tricking you and try to make things right.

2. Imagine you are the leader of a large group of people. One day, you decide to make a random rule without giving them a reason why. What will happen?

    A. They will accept your rule and follow it very closely.//
    B. They will break the rule and tease you about it.//
    C. They will break the rule secretly.//
    D. They will try to stop others who break the rule.//
    E. All of the above.

3. Say you never share the reason you made something against the rules with the people you lead, no matter how much they demonstrate they believe in you?

    A. More people will keep on following you closely.//
    B. More people will lose hope in you and break the rule.//
    C. Things will stay the same.

4. What will happen if you tell the people who enforce the rule you are proud of them, and they really helped you. Now they deserve to know the **true** reason for the rule and you will listen to their ideas.

    A. Most will accept your correct judgment and praise.//
    B. Most will be surprised because they were doing it to avoid getting in trouble. They were not trying to do the right thing.

5. What will happen if you tell the people who break the rule you are proud of them, and they should not follow rules that don't make sense without a reason. Now you will listen to their ideas.

    A. Most will accept your correct judgment and praise.//
    B. Most will be surprised because they were being naughty to make you mad for fun, and they were not really trying to do the right thing.

Answers:
1:B, 2:E, 3:B, 4:A, 5:A

Getting Along With Someone Who Is Nogentive

A **nogentive** person is a leader who has trouble working out how it would make the world a worse place to live if everyone supported their way.

They may choose to be not smart in thinking about how their ways affect the world for many (secret *) reasons:

- They are afraid to defy the caretakers who taught them their ways.
- They aren't close enough with their friends to suggest trying things a different way.
- They wouldn't even know how to say with *words* a suggestion for trying things a different way.
- They are not smart enough to plan out far ahead for ways that would take a long time to see a benefit.
- They don't have any control over how other people spend their time, so even if they thought of a better way, they could not get others to try it.
- People who have control of their time would not be interested, or would make them feel bad for wanting to try things a different way.
- They thought a **Self Guider** wouldn't want to see them struggle so hard getting along in this world, while also trying to change it for the better, so they gave up on changing it.
- They thought it would be too hard to make a difference.
- They were once a **Learner** who started play-thinking **nogentively** to see what their **nogentive** caretakers were dealing with, but something went wrong. Maybe they forgot why they started thinking like this. Now they keep on thinking like this.

* If you were once tricked by a **Pretending Person** and treated them like they were a great leader, but now you understand their secret reasons for doing things, then you might feel like telling them that you know all about their game. If you do, they might not understand your meaning at all and think you are getting angry for no reason. They and their friends have been pretending for so long, they have forgotten *why* they started pretending in the first place, or even that there could be **other ways** besides pretending. They may not even be smart enough to realize they tricked you.

Examples of things **nogentive** people do:

A **nogentive** sort of leader would take most of the candy from a bucket that says "Take one." If everyone did that, then the world would be a worse place because only a few people would get a lot of candy.

A **nogentive** sort of leader would think less of people when something bad happened to them that was outside of their control (like if they got sick and threw up in class). Since everyone has things that are outside of their control, people think less of others just based on luck instead of how hard they work.

A **nogentive** sort of leader would get mad at someone if they said "Sorry" all the time. Then they might get even madder when the person stopped saying sorry at all.

A **nogentive** sort of leader will make fun of people who make mistakes practicing skills in the open, and then get upset when they don't see as many people around anymore, since they have to practice alone to avoid being teased.

A **nogentive** sort of leader will get mad when people don't notice them for wearing something new, and will complain to **Learners** about it and make it seem like it was very wrong. The **Learners** might grow up to notice and talk to everyone who wears something new – even people who don't want to be noticed!

If a **nogentive** sort of leader takes a job they don't like, and **Learners** ask about it, they may yell, "DON'T ASK ABOUT MY JOB; THAT'S REALLY RUDE!!!" Now the **Learner** will never ask other **Learners** about their job, even though they both have a job they really like talking about. These **Learners** could even miss out on a chance to work together to make the world even better. The **nogentive** person would never realize the negative effect they had on the world.

How Do Some Things Get Rude?

Some actions are considered rude because there are **Bad Guys** in the world who do them to harm others. Someone saying something is "rude" could mean, "I don't know if you are a **Bad Guy** or not yet, so could you wait till I trust you more?" (Remember that **Wise Leaders** don't try to convince people they are trustworthy, they just accept the other person's judgment and continue to improve themselves.) They may not know why something is rude, just that it is. Examples:

1. Some **Workers** don't want to be near young **Learners** before their parents know them well.
2. Some people are afraid when others look up information about them because a **Bad Guy** could use it to steal money from their bank account.

Sometimes things get rude for other reasons. **Pretending People** who have control over how others spend their time make things rude to try to get even more control. **Nogentive** people support their changes because they can't tell what's going on. The world becomes a worse place for everyone, except for the **Pretending Person** in control of other people's time.

Example: The original reason it became rude if a man did not buy his wife a diamond ring was because of the people who sell diamonds. The **Pretending People** who sell diamonds paid other people to be in commercials, whose actions made it seem like they were saying, "It's definitely rude to not get your future wife a diamond ring, and she should be mad if she doesn't get one." Lots of nogentive and innatured people who depend on them believe it, and now most of the group follows the way of, "It's good to think it's rude if a husband doesn't buy his wife a diamond ring." The people who sell diamonds make lots of money, but they, and nogentive people who follow their way, never care to think, "Hmm… would the world be a better place if it wasn't considered rude?".

Exercise: On another piece of paper, mark a possible *real* reason a way is considered bad, which a **nogentive** person would be unable to think about and tell you.

1. You play some baseball before you go to school and your clothes are a bit dirty. A teacher yells at you to change. "But why?"

    A. The dirt would definitely make the other kids ill.

    B. People smarter than me decided it's bad.

    C. A long time ago, some people who were rich enough to clean their kids started the way of, "It's OK to **view** dirty kids as **less than** clean kids," so their own kids could receive more care. Now, I want you to be clean so you don't receive less care.

2. You ask your teacher, "Why don't you change the spelling of 'thumb' to 'thum'?"

    A. It's better this way.

    B. People smarter than me decided it would be for the best.

    C. I believe it's an important part of our culture.

    D. I don't have enough control over other people's time, so my suggestion to change the spelling will not be taken seriously. It's too hard for me to admit that. It's easier for me to think it's good this way.

3. You ask your teacher, "Why do you act like you know everything when you don't?"

    A. I never actually *said* I know everything. Kids always make that assumption, and it's always their fault.

B. I'm trying to communicate the idea that you shouldn't trust people, and this is the best way to communicate it.

C. I am not smart enough to act truthfully to kids. I don't actually know for sure if pretending is for the best or not. If I find any proof that it's not, I'm not smart enough to accept it.

Answers: 1:C, 2:D, 3:C

Pretending People's Thoughts About You

Pretending People have a very simplistic view of how you think. If you play recklessly and end up hurting yourself, instead of thinking, "It's nice that he is willing to take a little risk and is prepared to get hurt to gain skills *even faster*," they think, "He didn't expect to fall, and now he hurt himself, and since protecting the body is important, he did something dumb."

They may send you to do something that will take some time from your life and they say it's to help you. Unlike a **Wise Leader**, you can't trust they put a lot of time considering it, and you can't trust that they had your perspective in mind. They are probably doing it because someone else they look up to does stuff like that. If you let them know it went badly, they might do unexpected things, like get mad or call you a liar.

You might think that when they say they love you, they are willing to try anything to help you, even try things your way. They do not love you in this way, however. They love you in different ways that are difficult for them to describe because they cannot account for all their actions, like a **Self Guider**.

When **Pretending People** with the same ideas get together, they have a lot of influence on each other. They mostly focus on how people who don't see things their way are bad, without wondering if there is a reason to do things that way.

Since the only way to get along with a **Pretending Person** for long periods of time (besides sitting with them in silence) is trying things their way, you might start to become one. If you wish to be a **Wise Leader** someday, you might have to limit the contact you have with **Pretending People**. They might get very upset, but that's OK. The closer you are to being a **Wise Leader**, the more you can help future **Learners**. Even making one future **Learner** a little happy is better than making a **Pretending Person** happy. Maybe you can even return to the **Pretending Person** one day and help them.

Most of the ways they mistreat you have come from people they trusted when they were a **Learner**. If they misread your thoughts or feelings all the time, and are absolutely confident they are correct, you can be very sure that someone they trusted to be an **Everything Knower** misread their thoughts when they were little. Just about anything they do to you that is unpleasant was likely done to them by someone they trusted.

Talking to Friends About Pretending People

Don't call someone "a pretender" if you discover they are a **Pretending Person**. They are not **Pocobian** like a **Wise Leader**, so they will not understand your meaning. To them, it would feel the same as when someone calls you bad, when you are just trying your best.

It's important to speak about them in the way you would like to be spoken about too. Example conversation:

Kid 1: "I think they might be pretending to know everything."

Kid 2: "I think they might be pretending to guide themselves."

Kid 3: "I think they might be pretending to be a **Wise Leader**."

Kid 1: "When I discovered they didn't know something, instead of admitting it, they tried to hide it."

Kid 2: "When I found that they were not very talented at something I asked them to help me with, and I couldn't have known they weren't able, they called me dumb for not knowing they weren't talented in it."

Kid 3: "When it seemed clear they forgot something they did to me, they acted like they remembered."

Kid 2: "Are you sure they are not a **Learner** trying a different way?"

Kid 1: "I don't know. Maybe we need to be together more."

Kid 3: "If they are a **Pretending Person**, why do you think they are one?"

Kid 2: "Well, it's not because they are bad. Maybe it's because that is all they know."

Kid 1: "Maybe they are afraid that if they were honest with us, that we wouldn't listen to them?"

Kid 3: "Maybe something really bad happened to them when they were little with someone they thought was a **Self Guider**."

How a Learner Could Get Along With a Misguided Person

If they try to force you to act in a bad way, you should resist.

Sometimes, if they talk to you, they might try to do something that would make you forget the person you want to be or change you into someone else. They might use tricks, and say things like, "I used to feel the same way," or ask, "Are you chicken?"

Examples:

You: "Sorry, I don't want to smoke a cigarette."

Misguided Person: "Oh, I used to say the same thing. Then I tried it and everything was better."

You: "Sorry, I don't want to spy on people."

Them: "Oh, what are you? Chicken?"

You: "Sorry, I don't want to swim in that abandoned mine."

Them: "Don't you want to be Verse like a Self Guider? You gotta try everything once."

You: "Sorry, I don't want to boss these little kids around and hit them if they misbehave."

Them: "Don't worry; that's what they want you to do. They deserve it."

You: "Wow, this wrench tool is really new to me. I better be very careful when handling it until I'm more confident with it."

Them: "What are you? A baby? Ha ha."

Perhaps a way to talk to them would be to say ways (or principles) that a Wise Leader, Self Guider, or Everything Knower would think are important and perhaps worth spreading, or even worth fighting for.

You: "Sorry, I don't want to smoke a cigarette."

Misguided Person: "Oh, I used to say the same thing, then I

tried it and everything was better."

You: "Hmm, that's something to think about. OK, maybe I will **try it when I'm ready**, but that could take a long time." (Probably never.)

You: "Sorry, I don't want to spy on people."

Them: "Oh, what are you? Chicken?"

You: "No, I just think **people should not be seen if they don't want to be**."

You: "Sorry, I don't want to swim in that abandoned mine."

Them: "Don't you want to be Verse like a Self Guider? You gotta try everything once."

You: "Yea, but if something goes wrong, I could die. I think people **deserve to live**."

You: "Sorry, I don't want to boss these little kids around and hit them if they misbehave."

Them: "Don't worry; that's what they want you to do. They deserve it."

You: "I think people **deserve to be free**. Maybe I could get them to behave in a **peaceful** way."

You: "Wow, this wrench tool is really new to me. I better be very careful when handling it until I'm more confident with it."

Them: "What are you? A baby? Ha ha."

You: "No, I just think people should get a chance to **learn things at their own pace**."

Sometimes, you don't even need to tell them a reason, you just have to think it and then tell them something like: **"Naw, I don't want to do that, sounds really boring. Think I'll go do something else. Later."**

Sometimes, they act like they didn't hear you, act like you said you agreed to do what they wanted, or try to tell you how easy it would be to do what they want. You may have to **repeat yourself many times,** saying something like, "Well, as I just told you," then say what you said before, or tell them that your values are still the same since the last time they tried to convince you.

If they have been a **Misguided Person** for a long time, saying things like this might not work. You might have to say some things you learned in the chapter about how to get along with other **Learners**, in the section about what to do if you want to be left alone, starting on page 89. It covers options related to telling someone you want to be alone: negotiating with them, admitting your limits, telling them what kind of people you spend time with, threatening them, making fun of them, getting help, ignoring them, and using violence.

Spending a lot of time being cared for by a **Misguided Person** is unpleasant, to say the least. They hit, shout, call you names, use **Care Control Reasons**, and stare at you waiting until you do what they say. This can leave you confused and end up changing you into someone you don't want to be. Some people might make an imaginary world inside their head to escape life with a **Misguided Person** – once they are on their own, they won't be changed into another **Misguided Person**.

Sometimes, living in an imaginary world for so long can cause some problems, but may certainly be better than becoming another **Misguided Person**!

If you know that you live in a part of the world that recognizes a **Misguided Person's** ways as bad, you should find someone else to care for you. You can ask a **Worker** for help (especially **Workers** whose job it is to care for young **Learners**). You can tell them what's happening and they will ask you questions, and maybe get you some help. In this world, it is currently not recognized as bad to be a **Misguided Person**.

How a Learner Could Get Along With a Bad Guy

If a **Bad Guy** cares for you, you can be very sure that you can tell a **Worker** what's going on (especially **Workers** whose job it is to care for young **Learners**), and they will likely help you, especially if the damage that has been caused to you is easy to see!

You can run to almost any person you see and ask for help if you see a **Bad Guy** being bad!

Many people learn self-defense skills so they can defend themselves (and others) from **Bad Guys**. Some good guys like Police Officers use weapons to stop **Bad Guys**.

If you aren't able to use self-defense, or wish to use it only as a last resort, you can try using words. You can pretend to be their caretaker. Here are some things you can confidently say (or shout) to them:

"Leave me alone!"

"You need to leave here! Now!"

"I'm just a little girl/boy. You need to take care of me!"

"I know you don't want to do this. Let me go now!"

*This Police Officer found an interesting weapon to defeat **Bad Guys** with.*

How Other Types of People Get Along With and Communicate With Each Other

How to Get Along With a Worker If You Are a Worker

Talk about the weather. Talk about your day. Talk about plans and what to do in your spare time. Bring up your environment spaces, and how they are causing problems. You can talk about current events, and people that are causing problems, but don't talk about what kind of experiences in the past could have lead them to cause those problems. You ought to keep conversations light and steer clear of deep and important discussions.

If your ways are different from another Worker, don't try to resolve them, but avoid trying to talk about them.

If someone does something that, from your perspective, looks strange, then you can tell another Worker about it who would also think it's strange, to build friendship.

If you have just started getting to know another Worker pretty well, but then they have to move away, it's OK to be sad, but try not to be too sad. You'll probably meet someone else like them, and you could probably have the same types of experiences with different people.

Pretending Person Getting Along With a Wise Leader

If you are a Pretending Person trying to get along with a Wise Leader, you have several choices:

- Believe there is no such thing as Wise Leaders and this person is also Pretending, like you.
- Try to gain their favor to gain an advantage over others.
- Try to be a Learner again, and see if it goes well.

If you decide to be a Learner, read the part about the Learner and the Wise Leader.

If you decide to believe this person is also Pretending, see below:

Pretending Person Getting Along With Another Pretending Person

If you are a **Pretending Person** trying to get along with another **Pretending Person**, then you have two choices:

1. You can see them as an ally.
2. You can see them as an enemy.

It's OK to not put much thought into it. In some **Pretending Person** cultures, it's OK to decide based on if they made any mistakes the first time you met them.

If you want them to be your ally:

> Complain about something you both experienced. Talk about how other people's suffering or cries for help are very annoying to you. Complain about other people, without trying to understand them further.
>
> After they become your ally, you can talk about how to eliminate your common rivals. Sometimes, you don't even need to talk about it, and they will just follow your lead or you can follow theirs.

If you see them as a rival:

> Pretend to be their friend, but try to make it seem like you are better than them by saying something like: "Oh you're sooo good at *that*." If you are right about something and they were wrong, try to make them feel bad.

If they are your boss, you can try to look better by hurting your rivals. If hurting your rivals is easier than improving yourself and you won't get caught, you should always hurt your rivals. It doesn't matter if you are actually better, it only matters that you look better.

To be a Wise Leader Who Gets Along With a Learner

Be careful around **Learners**. Sometimes, they come up to you and announce how dedicated they are to a thing, or how much they like and believe in you. This actually means they are very dedicated to doing good, but have gotten very confused about what is actually good and what isn't. They have decided that you seem impressive enough to better guide them in achieving your good vision for the world. Be very cautious about what you do or say next because they will think very hard about it. Even if you don't intend to point them in a particular direction, they will try to work out a direction from your words or actions anyway. If people keep on disappointing them when they announce how dedicated they are, they might have to give up being a good member of the group, even though they would really have liked to! You should try to let them know your negative qualities, while also giving them something they could use to be better. They want you to think about all the good they could do to make a better world. It would be best that you do. They might even do more good than you one day!

Learners need to think a lot to figure out the world. Sometimes, they make little changes, either to see what happens or to make you happy. They pick from two options when not inventing their own actions:

1. Escalate: Take something you think is good, and add more.
2. Combine: Take two or more things you think are good and combine them into one thing.

There may be many reasons they would escalate and combine.

- Actions they make on their own always get a bad reaction. Escalating or combining things you think are good seems like something that would give rise to a good reaction.
- They intend to make their own actions, but to do that, it would take a long time. They could either sit alone and think about it, or escalate and combine with other ideas. They think you wouldn't want them to be sad, being all alone, so they choose to escalate and combine.

If a **Learner** sees you punch a **Bad Guy**, ignore a **Misguided Person**, or devalue a **Pretending Person's** time, you should explain why. Examples: "I only punched that **Bad Guy** because he was going to do something very bad," or "I only ignored that person because I tested them and found them to be **Misguided** and there were more needy **Learners** I needed to pay attention to." Then, they won't escalate or combine that way, unless it's under the **right setting**.

Learners are a very good investment of your time if your goals in life are noble. With money, you can invest in different stocks, some of which might be profitable, while others won't. Unlike money, **Learners** have the intelligence to let you know if you are investing **them** in a stock that won't pay out. They really want you to get the most out of the time and energy you invest in them.

If a **Learner** is doing something to upset you, you should think,

"What kind of messages would be so important that it would be worthwhile to upset someone, just to get a chance to communicate it?" You should really challenge yourself to think of what the most important messages could be. Of those messages, order them from **Most Good** and **Most Smart**, to **Most Good** and **Least Smart**. If you still have some ideas left over, order them from **Not so Good** and **Most Smart**, to **Not so Good** and **Least Smart**.

You can test to see if what they are thinking is true by playing with them and treating them like that was the message/reason they wanted you to know. If things work out well, then you did get the right message. If not, then you can do the same with the next idea on your list.

As you know, sometimes Learners like to try to help or ask questions but don't have the words to do it. They then may have to do something unpleasant as a way to say it. One thing they do is introduce the person to a lot of something that they think is scary, in the hope that they will notice how harmless it is.

Example: A Learner is playing with harmless leaves, but after they see you are scared of leaves, they get even more leaves to play with. They might be trying to **overexpose** you to scary leaves as a way to communicate that they think leaves are harmless. You could rethink how you feel about leaves and play with the Learner, or talk to the Learner about how it's nice that they are trying to help you, and maybe share some information about why leaves might actually be scary.

This Learner knows that leaves are harmless, but their Wise Leader friend doesn't think so. The Learner tried to help by throwing leaves at the Wise Leader till they understand too.

Sometimes, Learners put a lot of thought into deciding to do something. When they start doing it, they are so focused on getting it right that they forget *why* they decided to do it. You have limited power to change their past. You can alter the reasons why the Learner did something by how you respond to it. If you interpret them poorly, it may change them into a different person. Example: If they come up to you and show you how fast they can run, you shouldn't say things like, "Why are you practicing running? So you can get away when you steal stuff?" Instead, maybe you could say something like, "That's good to practice. Now you can catch a **Bad Guy** if you need to!" or "Now you can deliver presents super-fast!"

How to Get Along With a Wise Leader If You Are a Wise Leader

Even if you don't see yourself as a Wise Leader, it's good to practice getting along with one.

There are so few Wise Leaders in the world, that it might be best to sometimes treat people like they are **Workers**. After you have discovered enough clues that they might be a Wise Leader, you can start talking about stuff that might upset **Workers**, or bring up ideas that **Workers** don't like to think about.

After you figure it out, now it is OK to talk about what sort of experiences bad people might have gone through to become bad, and how to stop it from happening again. It is also OK to talk about how to use your advantages for good. You can also try to talk about what ways you have used on other people, and how things ended up.

With other Wise Leaders, you can plan ahead for what to do in different situations, so you don't get surprised if they actually happen.

- You could think about what you should do if one of your subjects decided to try a particular strategy, viewpoint, or way.
- You could think about what you should do if one of your subjects decided to focus on a particular job.
- You could ask each other questions like "Why do we even like doing things this way?" and, "Why don't we just try liking something that will help Learners more?".
- You could wonder if you are doing enough to help the world. What more could we do?
- You could plan what you would do if you met a **Bad Guy**.
- You could plan on what to do if something happened that

was outside of your control.

- You could try your best to plan what to do if something unplanned happened.
- You could plan on what you could do to keep the environment thriving without you.

You can think together with other **Wise Leaders**, "What kind of messages would be so important that it would be worthwhile upsetting someone to get a chance to communicate it?" If your subjects seem to act like your reasons aren't good enough, then oops, you might need a little help thinking of better reasons. You can ask your **Wise Leader** friends for help thinking of *even better* **Most Good** and **Most Smart** reasons, and try those.

Sometimes, there are settings where it's best if a group of people has no leader. Sometimes, there are settings where it's best if a group of people does have a leader. If having one leader is the way to go, then **Wise Leaders** can peacefully decide who among them would be best to lead because they want the best for everyone. They consider things like how **Verse**, limit-free, experienced, and good each one of them is. If one is chosen to be the leader, they will think, "This will be challenging because I will have to think very hard about how to help the most people, and I will be responsible for things that go wrong." If one is not chosen to be a leader, they will think, "This will be good because a better leader was chosen than me, and that will help more people!"

The End

www.ingramcontent.com/pod-product-compliance
Lightning Source LLC
Chambersburg PA
CBHW061232070526
44584CB00030B/4091